A-Z LEICES

D0313288

CONTENTS

REFERENCE

Motorway	**M1**
A Road	**A46**
Under Construction	
Proposed	
B Road	**B582**
Dual Carriageway	
One Way Street Traffic flow on A Roads is indicated by a heavy line on the driver's left.	→
Pedestrianized Road	
Restricted Access	
Track	
Footpath	
Residential Walkway	
Railway	Level Crossing Station
Built Up Area	MILL ST.
Local Authority Boundary	

Posttown Boundary By arrangement with the Post Office	
Postcode Boundary Within Posttowns	
Map Continuation	**10** Large Scale City Centre **4**
Ambulance Station	
Car Park	**P**
Church or Chapel	†
Fire Station	■
Hospital	**H**
House Numbers A & B Roads only	83 96
Information Centre	**i**
National Grid Reference	458
Police Station	▲
Post Office	★
Toilet with facilities for the Disabled	▽

SCALE

1:15,840
4 inches to 1 mile

0   1/4   1/2   3/4 mile

0   250   500   750   1 kilometre

Copyright of the Publishers Geographers' A-Z Map Company Ltd.

Head Office:
Fairfield Road, Borough Green, Sevenoaks, Kent, TN15 8PP
Telephone 01732 781000

Showrooms:
44 Gray's Inn Road, London, WC1X 8HX
Telephone 0171 242 9246

The Maps in this Atlas are based upon the Ordnance Survey 1:10,560 Maps
with the permission of the Controller of Her Majesty's Stationery Office.
© Crown Copyright.

Every possible care has been taken to ensure that the information given in
this publication is accurate and whilst the publishers would be grateful to
learn of any errors, they regret they cannot accept any responsibility for loss
thereby caused.

© 1996 Edition 4

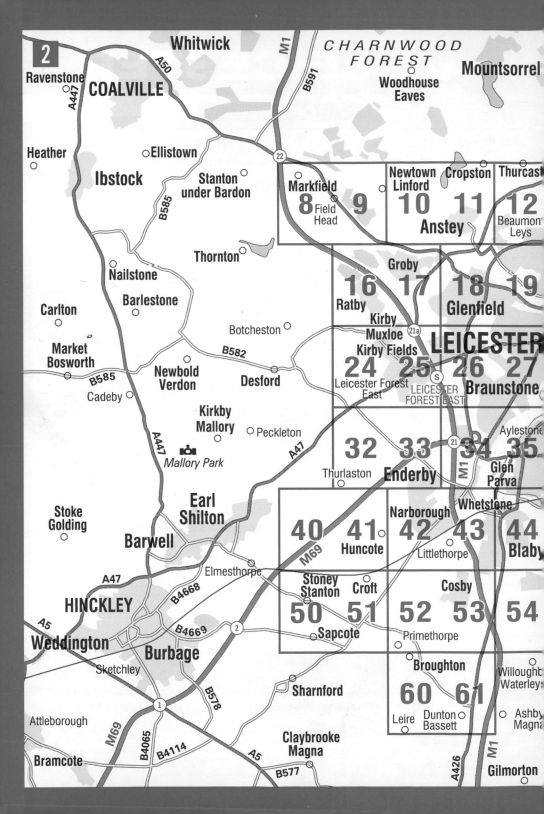

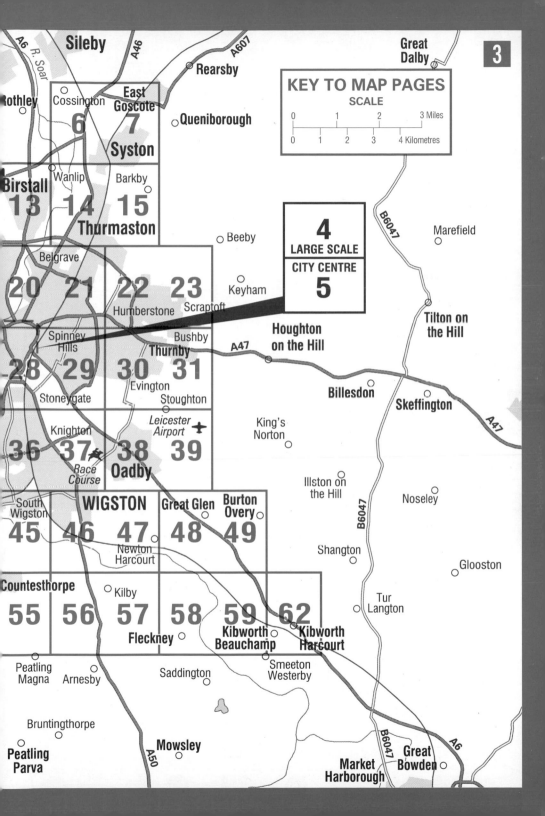

Sileby

R. Soar

Rearsby

Great Dalby

A46

A607

A6

Rothley

Cossington

East Goscote

6

7

Queniborough

Syston

KEY TO MAP PAGES

SCALE

| 0 | | 1 | | 2 | | 3 Miles |
| 0 | 1 | 2 | 3 | | 4 Kilometres | |

Birstall

Wanlip

Barkby

13

14

15

Thurmaston

Beeby

4

LARGE SCALE

CITY CENTRE

5

Marefield

B6047

Belgrave

20

21

22

23

Keyham

Humberstone

Scraptoft

Houghton on the Hill

Tilton on the Hill

Spinney Hills

Bushby

28

29

30

31

Thurnby

A47

Billesdon

Skeffington

A47

Stoneygate

Evington

Stoughton

Knighton

Leicester Airport ✈

King's Norton

36

37

38

39

Race Course

Oadby

Illston on the Hill

Noseley

B6047

South Wigston

WIGSTON

Great Glen

Burton Overy

45

46

47

48

49

Shangton

Glooston

Newton Harcourt

Countesthorpe

Kilby

Tur Langton

55

56

57

58

59

62

Fleckney

Kibworth Beauchamp

Kibworth Harcourt

Peatling Magna

Arnesby

Saddington

Smeeton Westerby

Bruntingthorpe

Mowsley

B6047

A6

Peatling Parva

A50

Market Harborough

Great Bowden

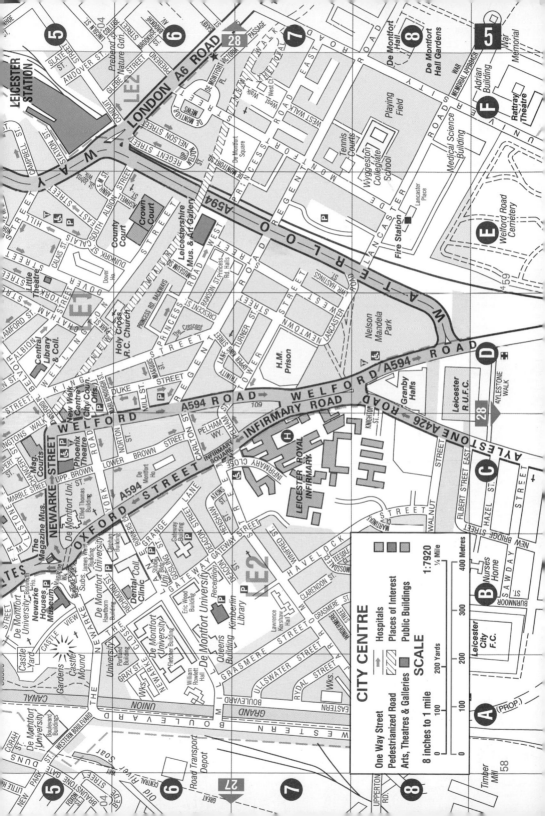

1

2

3

4

5

6

COSSINGTON ROAD

Brook Farm Nursery

Glebe Lodge Farm

Humbles Farm

Barn Lodge

Shepherds Crook

BLACKBERRY LANE

HUMBLE LANE

Home Farm

Cossington C.of E.Prim.Sch.

Rec.

Moat

HOMESTEAD CL.

CHURCH LA.

HUMBLE LANE

Lodge Farm

BENNETT'S LANE

BACK STREET

MIDDLEFIELD RD.

Drain

★ COSSINGTON

Short Lane Farm

Drain

PLATTS LANE

Pavilion

SYSTON

Grange Cottages

Cossington Grange

13

Marshdale Farm

Marshdale Farm

The Chestnuts

COSSINGTON ROAD

COSSINGTON A607

Depot

BY-PASS

A46

L   e   i   c   e

Towing Path

River   Wreake

Lock   Sluice

Weir

Weir

Weir Syston Mills

SYSTON

MILL LANE

Sludge Beds

C   H   A   R   N

12

Slipway

Marina

Boat Yard

Slipway

MEADOW

Barkby Brook

Boating Lake

Landing Stages

Grand Union Canal

Towing Path

WATER SPORTS CENTRE

BARKBY LANE

GLEBE WAY

WAY

GLEBE RD.

CURLEW

PARTRIDGE

KINGFISHER CL.

SWALLOW

WREN WAY

TEAL

SWIFT

MALLARD DR.

HERON WAY

NESTOR

SEWAGE WORKS

MARTIN

CYGNET

HOLLY CL.

BUSH CL.

ST. COLUMBA WAY

IONA

MOORLAND RD.

DOVINE

SWAN

WK.

BLACKTHORN

ROAD

Gravel Grading Plant

Pochin Bridge

SERGEIFIELD VW.

SPINNEY

HEATH

THE PADDOCK VW.

FRIDAY CL.

LINDISFARNE RD.

ABBOTS CL.

CRANMER DR.

CHATSWORTH

WESTERN A46

Barkby Spinney

Gravel Grading Plant

WANLIP

Wanlip Canal Bridge

PADDOCK

AV. WILLOW WK.

GORSE LA.

WAY

FOSSE WAY

WANLIP AV.

LEICESTER

River House

Manor Farm

Hall Farm

RECTORY RD.

Wanlip

Home Farm

⁴60

WATERMEAD PARK

Slipway

Boating Lake

WATER SPORTS CENTRE

Slipway

Warehouse

Warehouse

Pontylue Farm

Recreation Ground

ARCHDALE ST.

MAIDEN ST.

ST. ADAMS ST.

BRUXBY ST.

FOSSE WAY

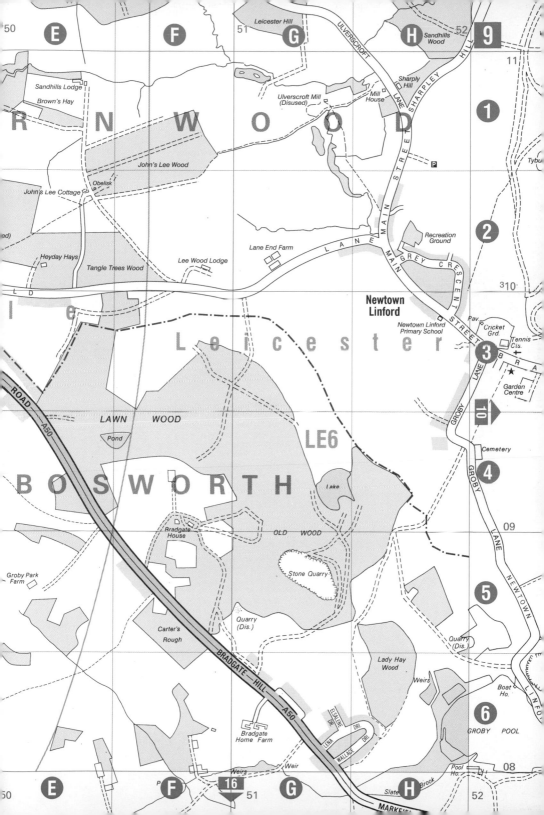

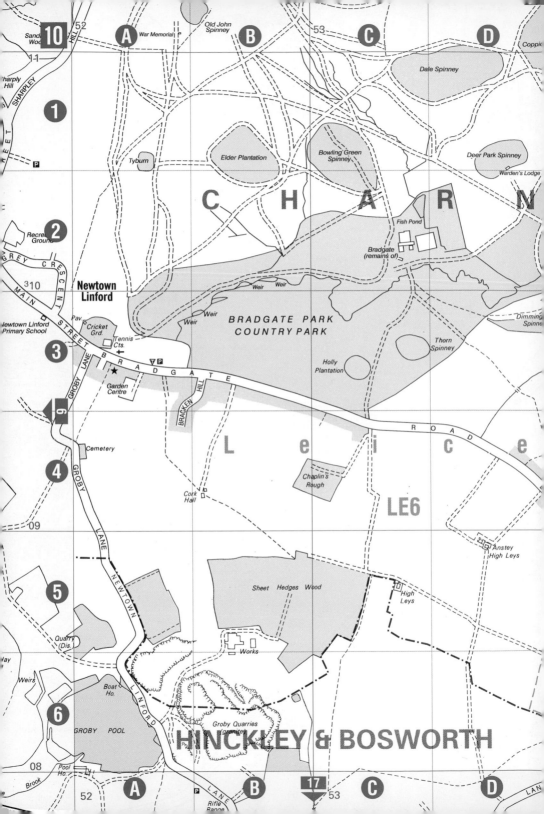

A · B · C · D

08

Coalville
LE67

1

Bradgate
Home Farm
9 51

Weirs · Weir

Pond

Groby Lodge
Farm

Slate · Brook

MARKFIELD · ROA
A50

Depot

Playing Field

Martinshaw County
Primary School

FERN · WOODLANDS · CRES

FERN CR.

Comm.
Cen.

FOREST
FAIRLANDS

FOREST CR.

2 M1
M1 · MOTORWAY

H I N C K

MARTINSHAW   WOOD

a n d

WOODBANK

HILL CR.

WYNWOOD

CR. CARMER

07

MARKFIELD

Lodge

Groby
Community
College

Brookvale
High School

Springf

3

B O S W O O

ROAD RA

SACH

4

L e i

THE POPLAR
BEVINGTON
CL.
CHARNWOOD
ASH · FARNWOOD
CL.
WOLSEY
STAMFORD

BRADGATE DR. RD
SQUIRES
WIN
WHITTINGTON
BRADGA
DRIVE
STAMFO

SAXONS
RISE

Vicarage

GROBY

COTTAGE
CLOSE · Overfield

Overfield

06

c e

Playing
Field

Ratby Prim.
Sch.

BURROUGHS
RD.

Library

MAIN · STREET

CHURCH LA.

CHURCH

WOODLEY RD.

OVERFIELD

FERNDALE

CLOSE

e

Bury Camp

5

LE6 RATBY

BERRY'S LA.

CHAPEL LA.

BELL CL.

INGLE DRI

WESLEY
CL.

CALVER-
TON CL.

GILLBANK

CARDINAL
CL.

GREEN
LEE RISE

DR.

NYMS
MEADOW

FREE·
MANS · DRI

ROBINS
FIELD

Playing
Field

Holywell Farm

GRANGE
CL.

TYLER

HEATHBROOK

MARTIN

RICHD

DRI

WINDMILL

BARTON

TAVERNER

JORDAN

6

LANE

STATION

ST. NICHOLAS

Pav.
Sports
Ground

Bus
Depot

Centurion Ct.

PARK RD.

MILL DRI.

Mill
House

CLIFF

WINDMILL

Conifers
Caravan
Park

Se.
Pu.
Sta.

Works

PARK

LE9

DESFORD

Works

3 05

450

Poultry
Houses

Playing
Field

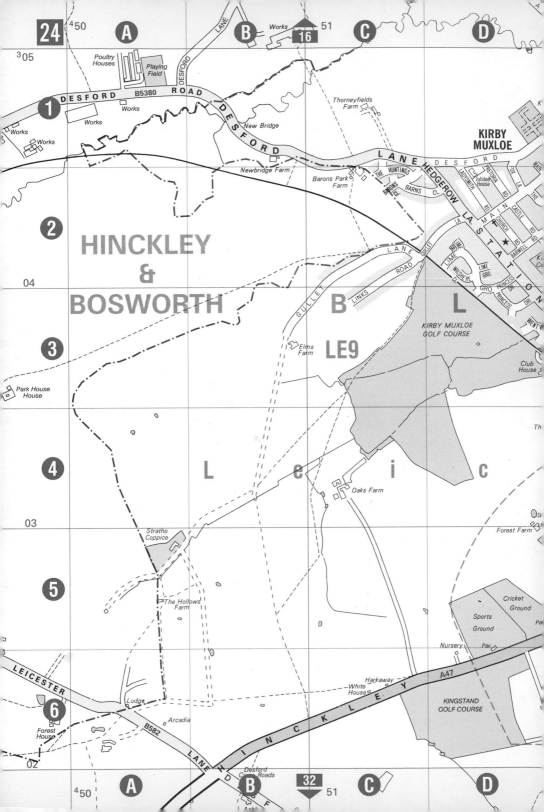

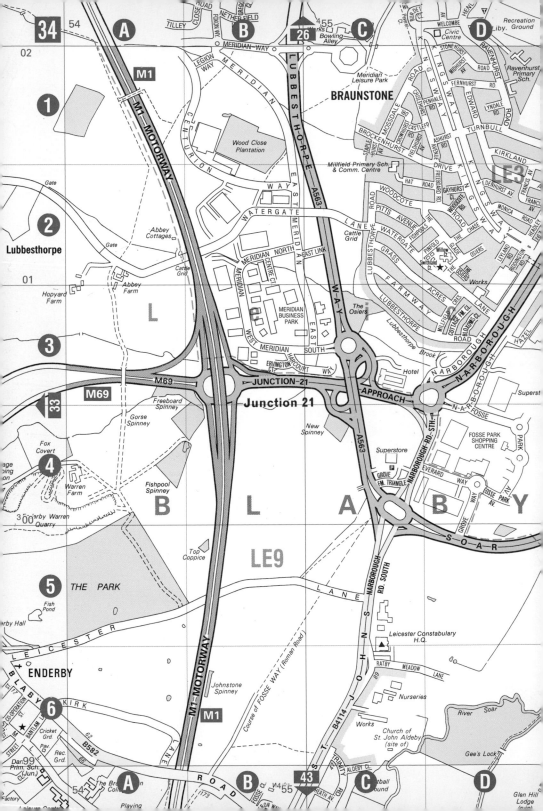

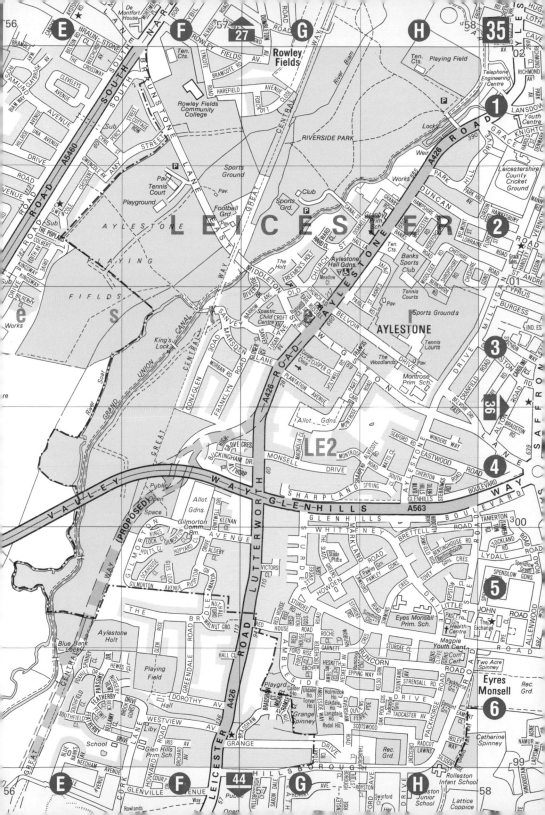

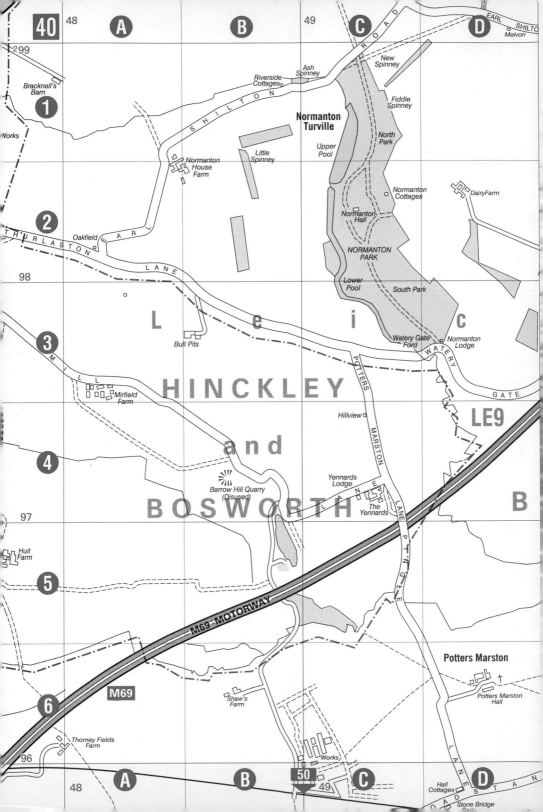

48
A
B
49
C
D

299

Earl Shilto
Melvon

Bracknell's
Barn

1

New
Spinney

Ash
Spinney

Riverside
Cottages

Fiddle
Spinney

Works

**Normanton
Turville**

North
Park

SHILTON

Little
Spinney

Upper
Pool

Normanton
House
Farm

Normanton
Cottages

DairyFarm

2

Oakfield

Normanton
Hall

THURLASTON

LANE

EARL

98

NORMANTON
PARK

Lower
Pool

South Park

3

Bull Pits

Watery Gate
Ford

Normanton
Lodge

MILL

L

e

i

C

WATERY

GATE

LE9

HINCKLEY

Mirfield
Farm

POTTERS

Hillview

MARSTON

4

Yennards
Lodge

and

Barrow Hill Quarry
(Disused)

The
Yennards

LANE

B

97

BOSWORTH

LANE

PINGLE

Huit
Farm

5

M69 - MOTORWAY

Potters Marston

6

M69

Potters Marston
Hall

Thorney Fields
Farm

Shaw's
Farm

Works

96

48
A
B

50
49
C

Hall
Cottages

D

STAN

ROAD

Stone Bridge

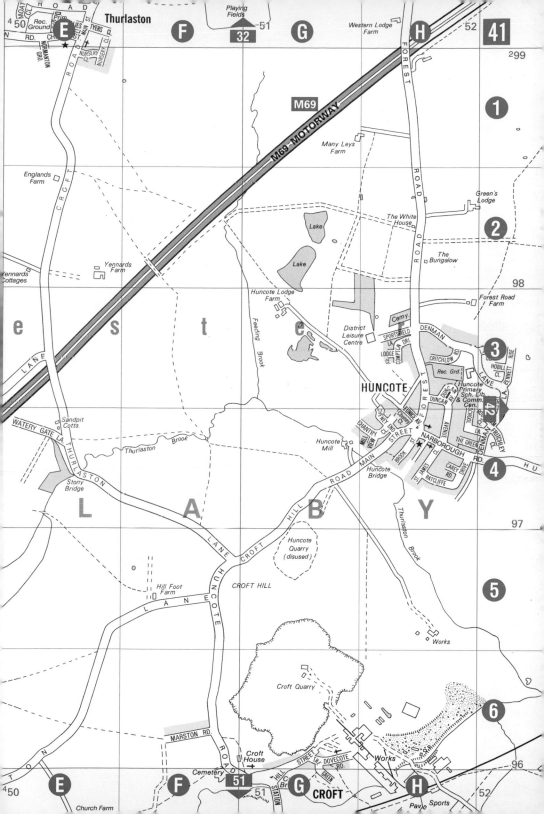

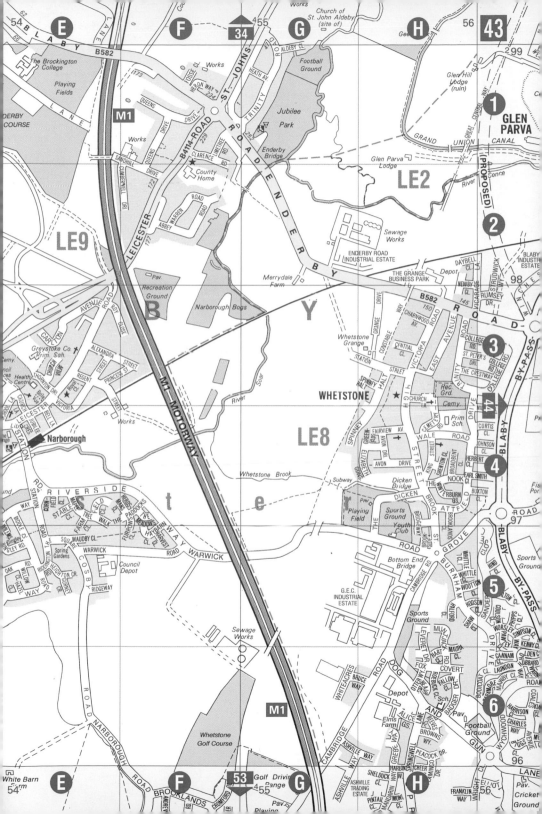

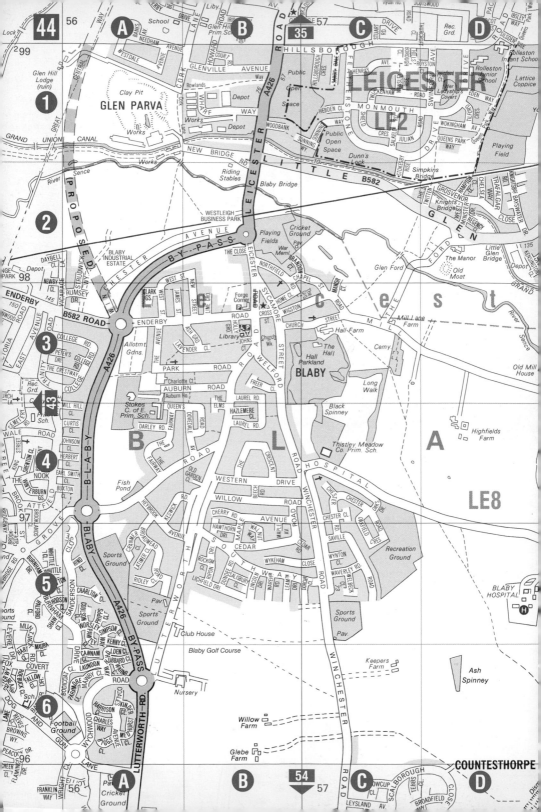

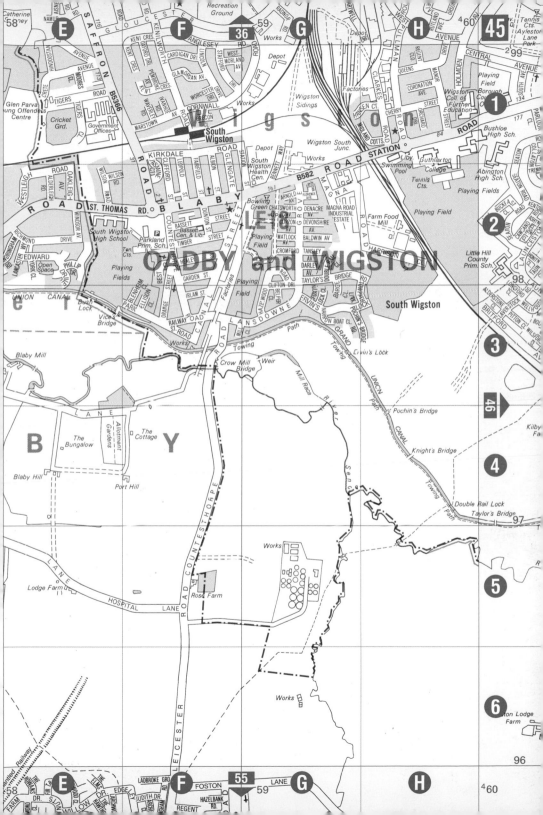

OADBY and WIGSTON

South Wigston

LE18

South Wigston Station

B582

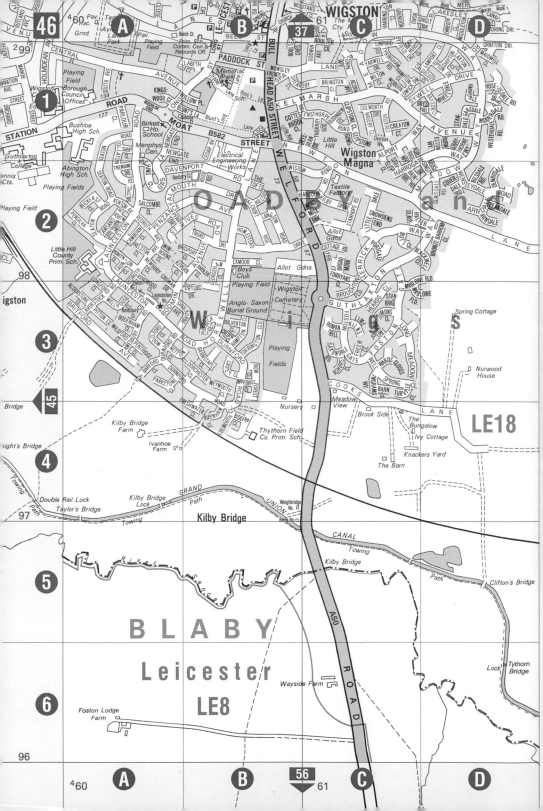

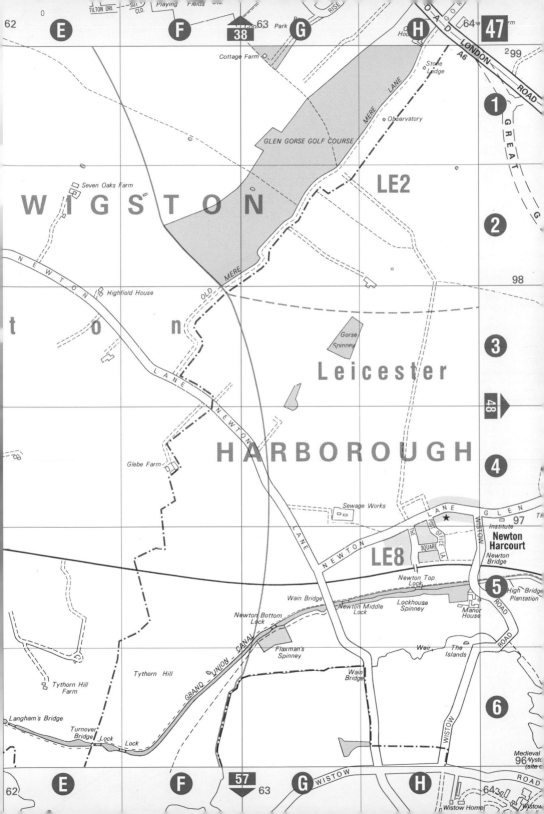

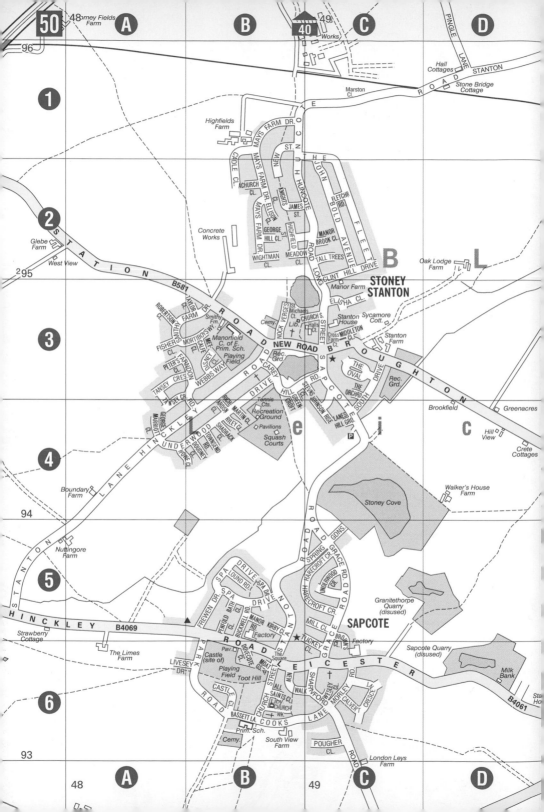

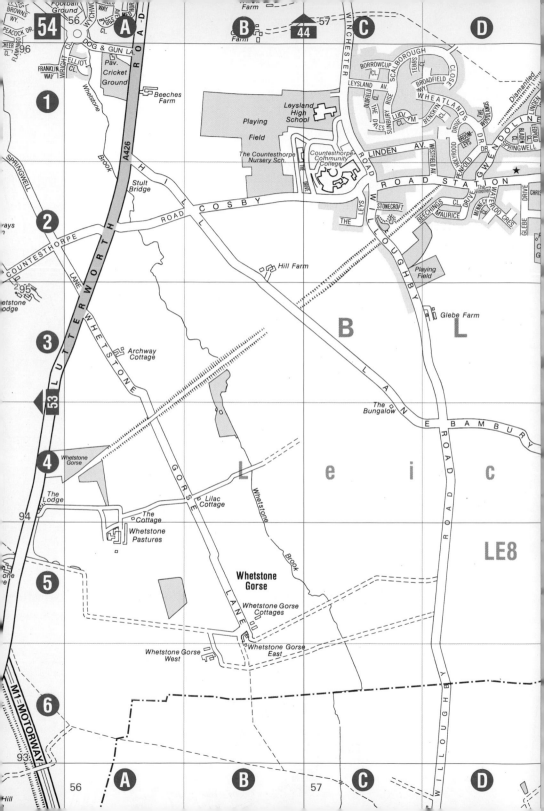

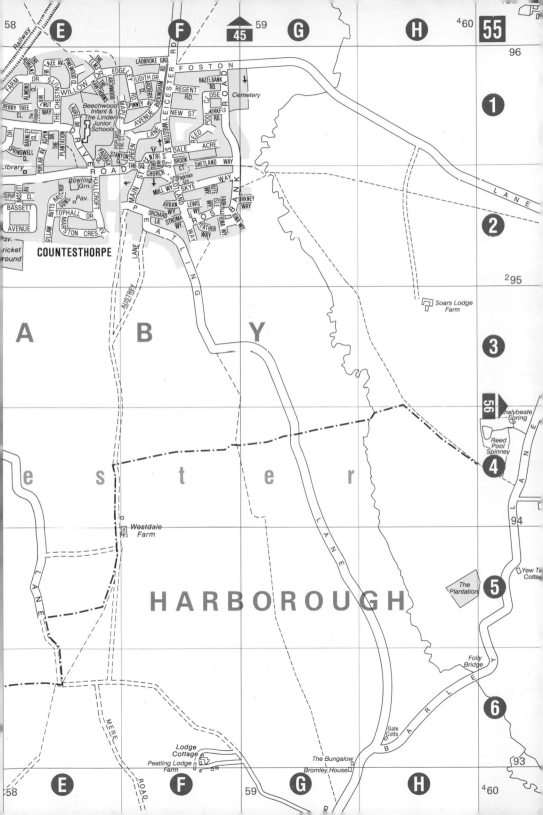

45

Railway

1

Cemetery

LEICESTER RD. FOSTON ROAD

Ladbroke Gro.
Edge
Judith Dr.
Hazelbank Rd.
Regent Rd.
Close
New St.
Kirkfield Rd.
Spinney Av.
Brockington
Beechwood Infant & The Linden Junior Schools
Maple Avenue
Reed Pool
Dale
Acre
Brook
Shetland Way
Church
The Sq.
Skye
Orkney Way
Packman Grn.
Scotland Way
Mull Way
Bute Way
Isle Way
Arran
Lewis
Stroma Wy.
Feather Way
Farm
Pinewood
Far Lee Av.
The Elms
Almond Dr.
Cherry Tree Cl.
Nut Way
The Chestnuts
Willow Dr.
Arrowood Dr.
Hartington Rd.
Springwell Av.
Poplar Av.
Aspen Cl.
The Dr.
Plantation
Barkley Cl.
DRIVE ROAD
Stanyon Paddock
Central St.
Main St.
Orchard La.
Gillam
Butts
Halcroft
Tophall Dr.
Weston Cres.
Hallcroft
Tophall
Pav.
Bowling Grn.
Library
Tophill
Bassett Cl.
Bassett Avenue
Guns.
Pav.

POSTLAND WY.
PREACHERS LANE

COUNTESTHORPE

2
2 95

Soars Lodge Farm

A **B** **Y**

3

56
Chalybeate Spring

Reed Pool Spinney

4
94

e s t e r

Westdale Farm

LANE

AUSTREY LANE
PEATLING LANE

H A R B O R O U G H

The Plantation

5
Yew Tr Cotta

Folly Bridge

BARLEY LANE

6
93

Gate Cotts.

MERE ROAD

Lodge Cottage
Peatling Lodge Farm

The Bungalow
Bromley House

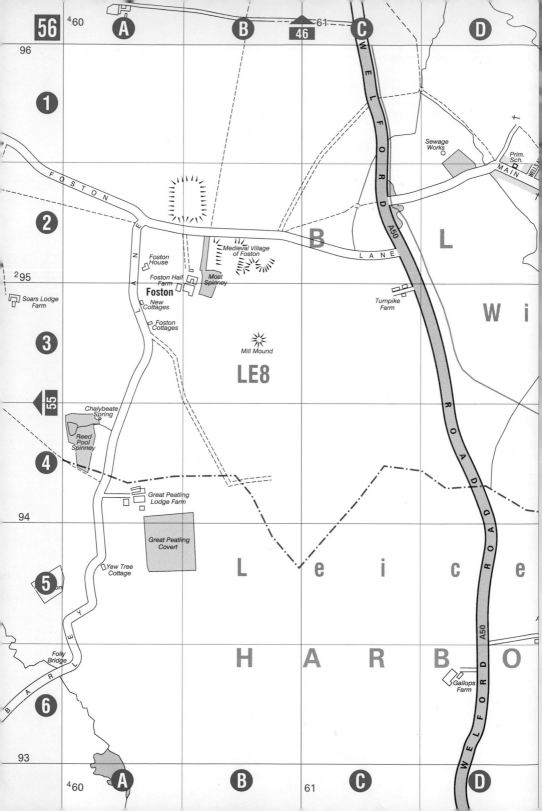

⁴60

A   **B**   ▲ 61   **C**   **D**

46

96

1

Sewage
Works

+
Prim.
Sch.

WELLS

MAIN

2

FOSTON

L

LANE

Medieval Village
of Foston

B

Foston
House

A50

Foston Hall
Farm

Moat
Spinney

W i

²95

Foston

New
Cottages

Turnpike
Farm

Soars Lodge
Farm

Foston
Cottages

3

Mill Mound

LE8

▲**55**

Chalybeate
Spring

Reed
Pool
Spinney

4

Great Peatling
Lodge Farm

94

Great Peatling
Covert

ROAD

L   **e i c e**

5

Yew Tree
Cottage

Folly
Bridge

BARLEY

A50

H A R B O

L

6

Gallops
Farm

WELFORD

93

⁴60   **A**   **B**   61   **C**   **D**

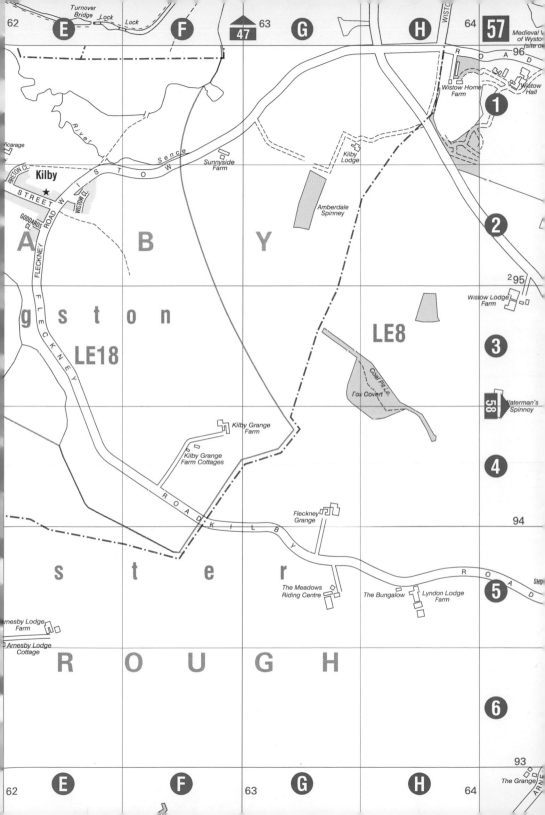

Vicarage

River

Sence

STOW

Kilby

BRETON CL

STREET

WISTOW CL

FLECKNEY ROAD

GODDARDS CL

Sunnyside Farm

Kilby Lodge

Amberdale Spinney

Wistow Home Farm

Wistow Hall

96

1

A B Y

95

2

Wistow Lodge Farm

g s t o n

LE18

FLECKNEY

LE8

Coal Pit La.

Fox Covert

3

58 Waterman's Spinney

Kilby Grange Farm

Kilby Grange Farm Cottages

4

ROAD KILBY

Fleckney Grange

94

s t e r

The Meadows Riding Centre

The Bungalow

Lyndon Lodge Farm

ROAD SHO

5

rnesby Lodge Farm

Arnesby Lodge Cottage

R O U G H

6

93

The Grange

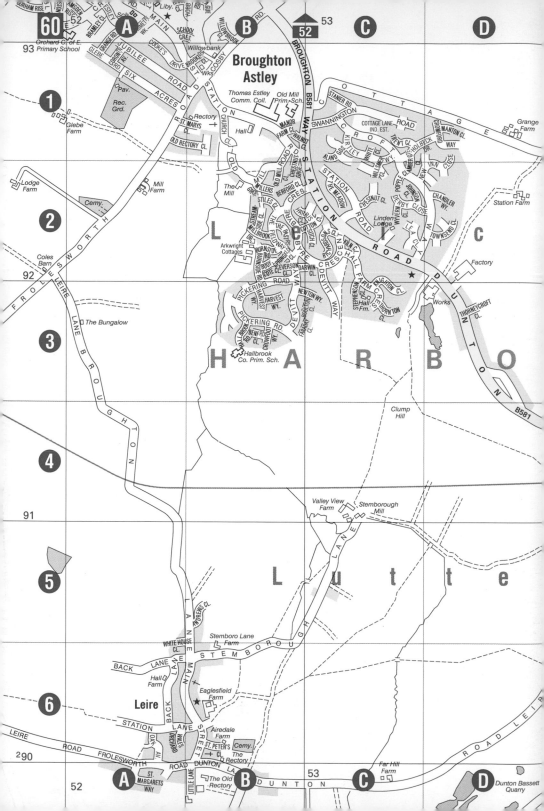

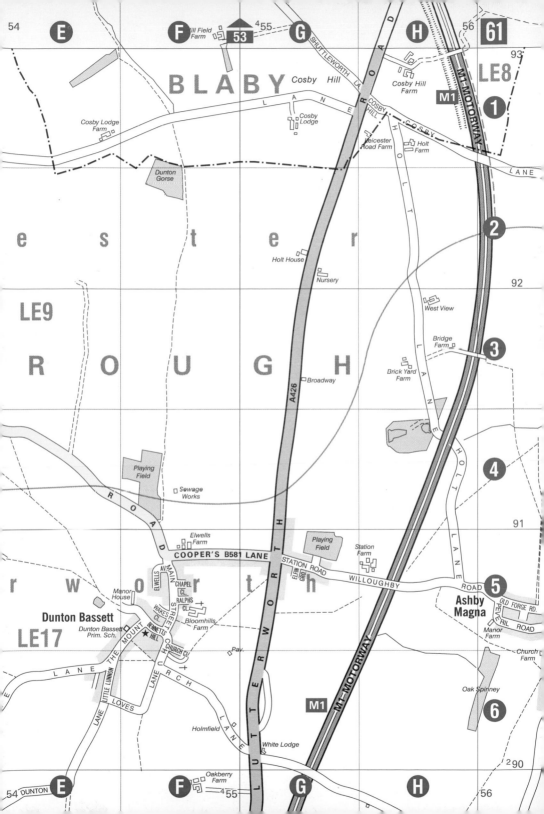

62

68   **A**   **B**   69   **C**   **D**   ⁴70

96

1

Reservoirs (Covered)   Carlton Clump

2

Glenfrith Hospital (Kibworth Hall)

²95

H A R B O R O U G H

Rifle Range

L e i c e s t e r

Sheepthorns Farm

3

Kibworth Harcourt

LEICESTER

ROCHESTER CL.

HALL

A6   MERTON WAY

MAIN   ALBERT   STREET   BEECH TREE CL.   BOROUGH CL.   WINNIFRED'S GDS.

SPINNEY   STREET   DR.

MARSH DRIVE

CARLTON   LANGTON   ROAD   KIBWORTH   ROAD

Windmill Farm   Windmill

LE8

4

HILL CRES.

R O A D   THE LEYS   HILLCREST — AVENUE

Kibworth C. of E. Prim. Sch.   St. WILFRID'S CL.   THE THINGS   THE VILLAS

CHURCH ROAD   RECTORY CL.   OAK TREE CL.   THE LANE   SOUTH LEA

Cemetery

94

STATION HOLLOW

PROSPECT RD.   MEADOWBROOK   MEADOWBROOK

Kibworth High Sch.   SCHOOL WALK   STATION ST.

ROOKERY CLOSE   BROOKFIELD WAY   LARKSWOOD

STREET   WHITE ST.   BULLER ST.   KIMBERLEY ST.   ROSEBERY ST.

SCHOOL RD.   PAGET ST.   Liby.   The Bank

Works

Works

STUART RD.

NEW   WEIR ROAD

5

HIGH   STREET

CEDAR CL.   VINE RD.

Hlth. Cen.

MORRISON CT.   HOME CL.

Recreation Ground

Beaufield Farm

Kibworth CL.

LINKS ROAD   PADDOCK THE   GRANGE DRIVE   GRANGE CL.   CRANMER CL.   FAIRWAY   FAIRWAY   BIRDIE CL.

BRAUNSTONE MILE   MARKFIELD CL.   STONE DR.   TABLE CL.

Hatchery

6

SPRINGFIELD THE   SPRINGFIELD CL.   SPRINGFIELD CRES.

Kibworth Beauchamp

Sewage Works

WEST   LANGTON   ROAD

Kibworth High Sch. & Community Centre

SMEETON ROAD

S. GRANARY CL.

Club House

A6   ROAD

Masons Farm

Smeeton Westerby

93

LANE   BLACK SMITHS LA.   MAIN ST.   SPRINGFIELD LA.   Springfield Farm

A   **B**   GOLF   COURSE   **C**   **D**

69   ⁴70

INDEX TO STREETS

HOW TO USE THIS INDEX

1. Each street name is followed by its Posttown or Postal Locality and then by its map reference; e.g. Abbey Pk. Rd. Leic —4A **20** is in the Leicester Posttown and is to be found in square 4A on page **20**. The page number being shown in bold type.
   A strict alphabetical order is followed in which Av., Rd., St., etc. (though abbreviated) are read in full and as part of the street name; e.g. Abbeycourt Rd. appears after Abbey Ct. but before Abbey Dri.

2. Streets and a selection of Subsidiary names not shown on the Maps, appear in the index in *Italics* with the thoroughfare to which it is connected shown in brackets; e.g. *Chesterton Wlk. Leic —2E* **27** *(off Gaskell Wlk.)*

3. The page references shown in brackets indicate those streets that appear on the large scale map pages **4** & **5**;
   e.g. Abbey St. Leic —6B **20** (1D **4**) appears in square 6B on page **20** and also appears in the enlarged section in square 1D on page **4**.

GENERAL ABBREVIATIONS

All : Alley
App : Approach
Arc : Arcade
Av : Avenue
Bk : Back
Boulevd : Boulevard
Bri : Bridge
B'way : Broadway
Bldgs : Buildings
Bus : Business
Cen : Centre
Chu : Church
Chyd : Churchyard
Circ : Circle
Cir : Circus

Clo : Close
Comn : Common
Cotts : Cottages
Ct : Court
Cres : Crescent
Dri : Drive
E : East
Embkmt : Embankment
Est : Estate
Gdns : Gardens
Ga : Gate
Gt : Great
Grn : Green
Gro : Grove
Ho : House

Ind : Industrial
Junct : Junction
La : Lane
Lit : Little
Lwr : Lower
Mnr : Manor
Mans : Mansions
Mkt : Market
M : Mews
Mt : Mount
N : North
Pal : Palace
Pde : Parade
Pk : Park
Pas : Passage

Pl : Place
Rd : Road
S : South
Sq : Square
Sta : Station
St : Street
Ter : Terrace
Up : Upper
Vs : Villas
Wlk : Walk
W : West
Yd : Yard

POSTTOWN AND POSTAL LOCALITY ABBREVIATIONS

Ans : Anstey
Ash M : Ashby Magna
Ash P : Ashby Parva
Ayl : Aylestone
Bark : Barkby
Belg : Belgrave
Bir : Birstall
Blab : Blaby
Braun : Braunstone
B Ast : Broughton Astley
Bur O : Burton Overy
Bush : Bushby
Cosb : Cosby
Costn : Cossington
Count : Countesthorpe

Cft : Croft
Crop : Cropston
Des : Desford
Dun B : Dunton Basset
Earl S : Earl Shilton
E Gos : East Goscote
End : Enderby
Evi : Evington
Flec : Fleckney
Glen : Glenfield
Glen P : Glen Parva
Gl G : Great Glen
Grob : Groby
Ham : Hamilton
Hum : Humberstone

Hunc : Huncote
Kib : Kibworth
Kilb : Kilby
Kir M : Kirby Muxloe
L'thrpe : Littlethorpe
Leic : Leicester
Leic F : Leicester Forest East
Leir : Leire
Mark : Markfield
Nar : Narborough
New H : Newton Harcourt
New L : Newtown Linford
Oad : Oadby
Pot M : Potters Marston
Quen : Queniborough

Rat : Ratby
Sad : Saddington
Sap : Sapcote
Scrap : Scraptoft
Sm W : Smeeton Westerby
Sto S : Stoney Stanton
Stoug : Stoughton
Sys : Syston
Thurc : Thurcaston
Thurl : Thurlaston
Thurm : Thurmaston
Thurn : Thurnby
Wan : Wanlip
Whet : Whetstone
Wig : Wigston

INDEX TO STREETS

Abbey Bus. Pk. Leic —6A **20**
Abbey Ct. Leic —3B **20**
Abbeycourt Rd. Leic —2B **20**
Abbey Dri. Leic —2B **20**
Abbey Ga. Leic —6A **20**
Abbey Ho. Leic —5F **19**
Abbey La. Leic —4A **20**
Abbey Meadows. Leic —4B **20**
Abbeymead Rd. Leic —2B **20**
Abbey Pk. Rd. Leic —4A **20**
Abbey Pk. St. Leic —5C **20**
Abbey Rise. Leic —2B **20**
Abbey Rd. Nar —2F **43**
Abbey St. Leic —6B **20** (1D **4**)
Abbey Wlk. Leic —6B **20**
Abbots Clo. Leic —5B **22**
Abbots Ct. Leic —5B **22**
Abbotsford Clo. Scrap —5F **23**
Abbotsford Rd. Leic —6H **21**

Abbots Rd. Leic —5B **22**
Abbotts Clo. Sys —6D **6**
Aberdale Rd. Leic —4D **36**
Aber Rd. Leic —5F **29**
Aber Wlk. Leic —5F **29**
Abingdon Rd. Leic —3D **28**
Abney St. Leic —3E **29**
Acacia Av. Bir —3H **13**
Acacia Clo. Leic F —5F **25**
Acan Way. Nar —4C **42**
Acer Clo. Leic —1G **19**
Acer Clo. Nar —4C **42**
Achurch Clo. Sto S —2B **50**
Acorn St. Leic —3D **20**
Acorn Way. Leic —5F **29**
Acres Rd. Leic F —4G **25**
Adcock Rd. Leic —6F **19**
Adderley Rd. Leic —5C **28**
Adlington Rd. Oad —3C **38**

Agar St. Leic —4D **20**
Aigburth. Oad —1A **38**
Aikman Av. Leic —5D **18**
Aikman Clo. Leic —6E **19**
Ainsdale. Flec —6C **58**
Ainsdale Rd. Leic —2E **27**
Ainsworth Wlk. Leic —2E **27**
Aintree Clo. Leic —2D **30**
Aintree Cres. Oad —3H **37**
Aisne Rd. Wig —6A **36**
Alan Clo. Leic —1D **20**
Aland Gdns. B Ast —1C **60**
Albany, The. Leic —4E **29**
Albemarle Hall. Leic —5A **22**
Alberta St. Leic —1D **28**
Albert Rd. Leic —5E **29**
Albert St. Flec —5B **58**
Albert St. Kib —3A **62**
Albert St. Sys —6F **7**

Albion Pde. Sys —6F **7**
Albion St. Ans —5G **11**
Albion St. Leic —2B **28** (5D **5**)
Albion St. Oad —4A **38**
Albion St. Sys —6F **7**
Albion St. Wig —1F **45**
Alcester Dri. Leic —3D **30**
Aldeby Clo. Leic —5F **35**
Aldeby Clo. Nar —1G **43**
Alder Clo. Leic F —5F **25**
Alder Gro. Est. Nar —1C **42**
Alderleigh Rd. Glen P —2E **45**
Alderstone Clo. Wig —3A **46**
Alderton Clo. Leic —6A **14**
Aldgate Av. Leic —4B **30**
Alexander Av. End —6G **33**
Alexander St. Leic
                    —1A **28** (3A **4**)
Alexandra Ct. Oad —4B **38**

Alexandra Rd. Leic —6F **29**
Alexandra St. Nar —3E **43**
Alexandra St. Thurm —3C **14**
Alfred Pl. Leic —2C **28** (4E **4**)
Alfreton Rd. Wig —5E **37**
Alice Gdns. Whet —6H **43**
Allandale Rd. Leic —6G **29**
Allenwood Rd. Leic —5A **36**
Allexton Gdns. Leic —1B **26**
Alliance Rd. Glen —6A **18**
Allington Dri. Bir —2H **13**
Allington St. Leic —5D **20**
Allinson Clo. Leic —1A **30**
Alloway Clo. Leic —1F **21**
All Saints Clo. Sap —6B **50**
All Saints Open. Leic
—1A **28** (2A **4**)
All Saints Rd. Leic
—1A **28** (2A **4**)
All Saints Rd. Thurc —1B **12**
Alma St. Leic —6G **19**
Almond Clo. Count —1E **55**
Almond Rd. Leic —4B **28**
Alport Way. Wig —1C **46**
Altar Stones La. Mark —1A **8**
Althorp Clo. Leic —4F **35**
Alton Rd. Leic —4A **36**
Alvaston Rd. Leic —6F **27**
Alvecote Rd. Leic —4G **35**
Alyssum Way. Nar —2B **42**
Amadis Rd. Leic —1E **19**
Amanda Rd. Leic —5F **35**
Ambassador Rd. Leic —1A **30**
Ambassador Wlk. Leic —1D **30**
Amber Ga. Clo. B Ast —2C **60**
Ambergate Dri. Bir —3F **13**
Amberley Clo. Thurm —5C **14**
Ambler Clo. Wig —2B **46**
Ambleside Clo. Leic —6G **35**
Ambleside Dri. Leic —6G **35**
Ambleside Way. Leic —6G **35**
Ambrose Clo. Leic —1F **27**
Amersham Rd. Leic —4H **19**
Amesbury Ct. Wig —3A **46**
Amesbury Rd. Wig —3A **46**
Amhurst Clo. Leic —4D **18**
Amos Rd. Leic —1B **26**
Amsden Rise. B Ast —6H **51**
Amyson Rd. Leic —1C **30**
Amy St. Leic —1E **35**
Anchor St. Leic —3B **20**
Andover St. Leic
—2C **28** (5F **5**)
Andrew Av. Cosb —1F **53**
Andrewes Clo. Leic —2H **27**
Andrewes St. Leic —2H **27**
Andrewes Wlk. Leic —2H **27**
Andrew Rd. Ans —5G **11**
Andrews Clo. Leir —5B **60**
Aneford Rd. Leic —4G **21**
Angela Dri. Leic —3B **30**
Anglesey Rd. Wig —6B **36**
Angus Clo. Thurn —1F **31**
Ann St. Leic —1C **28** (3F **4**)
Ann's Way. Oad —4C **38**
Anstey La. Ans & Leic —1C **18**
Anstey La. Grob —2G **17**
(in two parts)
Anstey La. Thurc —3H **11**

Anthony Dri. Thurn —2F **31**
Anthony Rd. Leic —4H **19**
Apollo Clo. Leic —2D **28**
Apollo Ct. Leic —2D **28**
Appleby Clo. Leic —2A **26**
Appleby Rd. Thurm —4E **15**
Applegate. Leic —2A **28** (4B **4**)
Appleton Av. Leic —1H **19**
Approach, The. Leic —3H **29**
Aquitaine Clo. End —6G **33**
Arbour Rd. Cft —1G **51**
Arbour Rd. Leic —3D **20**
Arcade, The. Wig —6F **37**
Archdale St. Sys —6D **6**
Archdeacon La. Leic —6B **20**
Archer Clo. Leic —1G **21**
(in two parts)
Archers Grn. E Gos —2H **7**
Archery Clo. Count —1F **55**
Archway Rd. Leic —4E **23**
Ardath Rd. Leic —4E **21**
Arden Av. Leic —6D **26**
Ardern Ter. Leic —5F **27**
Arkwright Cotts. B Ast —2B **60**
Armadale Dri. Leic —5C **22**
Armadale Grn. Leic —5C **22**
Armson Av. Kir M —2E **25**
Armston Rd. Cosb —2F **53**
Arncliffe Rd. Leic —5C **22**
Arndale. Wig —2D **46**
Arnesby Cres. Leic —4B **36**
Arnesby Rd. Flec —6A **58**
Arnhem St. Leic —2C **28** (5E **5**)
Arnold Av. Wig —2G **45**
Arnold Clo. Cosb —3F **53**
Arran Rd. Leic —1F **21**
Arran Way. Count —2F **55**
Arreton Clo. Leic —2E **37**
Arum Way. Leic —1B **26**
Arundel St. Leic —2H **27**
Ascot Rd. Leic —3D **20**
Asfordby St. Leic —1F **29**
Asha Margh. Leic —3C **20**
Ashbourne Rd. Wig —5E **37**
Ashbourne St. Leic —2E **29**
Ashby Rise. Gt G —2D **48**
Ashby Rd. Mark —1B **8**
Ash Clo. Rat —4B **16**
Ashclose Av. Leic —2E **37**
Ashdown Av. Leic —1F **27**
Ashdown Rd. Wig —5F **37**
Ash Dri. Sys —1F **15**
Ashfield Dri. Ans —6F **11**
Ashfield Rd. Leic —4E **29**
Ashfield Rd. Thurm —3D **14**
Ashford Ct. Leic —6F **29**
Ashford Rd. Leic —6C **28**
Ash Gro. Blab —3B **44**
Ashington Clo. Leic —5F **19**
Ashlands Way. Nar —2B **42**
Ashleigh Ct. Glen —5A **18**
Ashleigh Gdns. Leic —4G **27**
Ashleigh Rd. Glen —5H **17**
Ashleigh Rd. Leic —3G **27**
Ashlyns Rise. Leic —2C **26**
Ashmead Cres. Bir —2A **14**
Ashover Clo. Cosb —1F **53**
Ashover Rd. Leic —3F **29**

Ash Rd. Cft —2H **51**
Ash St. Leic —6E **21**
Ashthorpe Rd. Leic —3E **27**
Ashton Clo. Oad —6B **38**
Ashton Clo. Wig —2A **46**
Ash Tree Clo. Oad —5B **38**
Ash Tree Rd. Cosb —2F **53**
Ashtree Rd. Ham —3C **22**
Ash Tree Rd. Oad —5B **38**
Ashurst Clo. Wig —3C **46**
Ashurst Rd. Leic —1D **34**
Ashville Trading Est. Whet
—1H **53**
Ashville Way. Whet —1G **53**
Ashwell St. Leic —3C **28** (6E **5**)
Askrigg Way. Wig —1C **46**
Aspen Dri. Count —1E **55**
Asplin Rd. Leic —4A **36**
Asquith Boulevd. Leic —4C **36**
(in four parts)
Asquith Way. Leic —4C **36**
Astill Dri. Leic —1B **20**
Astill Lodge Rd. Leic —5A **12**
Astley Clo. Leic —4F **27**
Aston Hill. Leic —1C **36**
Atherstone Clo. Oad —4D **38**
Atkinson St. Leic —1F **29**
Atkins St. Leic —3B **28** (6C **5**)
Atlas Clo. Leic —2D **28**
Attfield Dri. Whet —4H **43**
Attingham Clo. Leic —5F **21**
Attlee Way. Leic —4A **36**
Auburn Ho. Blab —3A **44**
Auburn Ho. Leic —6E **19**
Auburn Rd. Blab —3A **44**
Auden Clo. Leic —3F **19**
Audley End. Leic —6F **27**
Augusta Clo. Leic —2A **26**
Augustus Clo. Sys —1C **14**
Austin Rise. Leic —5D **22**
Austrey La. Count —3F **55**
Austwick Clo. Leic —2G **19**
Avebury Av. Leic —4G **19**
Avenue Clo. Quen —4H **7**
Avenue Gdns. Leic —6E **29**
Avenue Rd. Leic —6E **29**
Avenue Rd. Quen —4H **7**
Avenue Rd. Extension. Leic
—6C **28**
Avenue, The. Blab —3A **44**
Avenue, The. B Ast —6A **52**
Avenue, The. Glen —4H **17**
Avenue, The. Leic —5E **29**
Averill Rd. Leic —1B **30**
Avery Dri. Mark —2B **8**
Avery Dri. Sys —4F **7**
Avery Hill. Leic —3B **26**
Avoca Clo. Leic —1B **30**
Avon Clo. Oad —4C **38**
Avondale Rd. Wig —6F **37**
Avon Dri. Whet —4H **43**
Avon Rd. Leic —5C **26**
Avonside Dri. Leic —2H **29**
Avon St. Leic —3D **28**
Axbridge Clo. Leic —4H **19**
Aylesham Ct. Leic F —4F **25**
Aylestone Dri. Leic —4H **35**
Aylestone La. Wig —5C **36**

Aylestone Rd. Leic
—3G **35** (8C **5**)
Aylestone Wlk. Leic —4B **28**
Aylmer Rd. Leic —3D **26**
Ayscarth Rd. Leic —2G **19**
Ayston Rd. Leic —6E **27**

Babingley Dri. Leic —3H **19**
Babington Row. Leic —4C **36**
Back La. Bur O —2H **49**
Back La. Costn —2B **6**
Back La. Leir —6A **60**
(in two parts)
Baddeley Dri. Wig —5D **36**
Baden Rd. Leic —4G **29**
Badger Dri. Whet —6H **43**
Badgers Clo. Leic —2F **19**
Badgers Clo. Nar —4C **42**
Badger's Corner. E Gos —1H **7**
Badgers Holt. Oad —5A **38**
Badminton Rd. Leic —6B **14**
Badminton Rd. Sys —4F **7**
Baggrave St. Leic —1F **29**
Baileys La. Bur O —1H **49**
Bainbridge Rd. Leic —6F **27**
Bainbridge Rd. Wig —2C **46**
Baines La. Leic F —4H **25**
Bakery Clo. Cosb —3F **53**
Bakewell Rd. Wig —5E **37**
Bakewell St. Leic —2E **29**
Bala Rd. Cft —1H **51**
Balcombe Av. Leic —1F **27**
Balderstone Clo. Leic —2A **30**
Baldwin Av. Wig —2G **45**
Baldwin Rise. B Ast —6H **51**
Baldwin Rd. Leic —4D **36**
Bale Rd. Leic —4G **21**
Balfour St. Leic —6H **19**
Balisfire Gro. Leic —2F **19**
Balk, The. Glen —4H **17**
Balladine Rd. Ans —4G **11**
Ballards Clo. Leic —2F **19**
Ballater Clo. Leic —4D **30**
Balliol Av. Sys —1G **15**
Balmoral Clo. Leic —2E **37**
Balmoral Dri. Leic —5C **26**
Bambury La. Count —4D **54**
Bambury Way. Leic —3C **36**
Bampton Clo. Wig —3B **46**
Bankart Av. Leic —6G **29**
Bankside. Leic —5E **23**
Banks Rd. Leic —2H **35**
Banks, The. Cosb —3F **53**
Bank, The. Count —1F **55**
Bank, The. Kib —5A **62**
Bannerman Rd. Leic —4F **29**
Bantlam La. End —6H **33**
Barbara Rd. Leic —6B **22**
Barbara Av. Leic F —4E **25**
Barbara Clo. End —6G **33**
Barbara Clo. Leic —6F **27**
Barclay St. Leic —3G **27**
Bardolph St. Leic —5D **20**
Bardolph St. E. Leic —5E **21**
Barfoot Clo. Flec —4A **58**
Barfoot Rd. Leic —4B **36**
Barford Clo. Wig —3A **46**
Barge Clo. Wig —3G **45**

Barkby Holt La. Bark —3H **15**
Barkby La. Sys —1D **14**
Barkby Rd. Leic —3F **21**
Barkby Rd. Quen —6H **7**
Barkby Rd. Sys —5F **7**
Barkby Thorpe La. Thurm &
  (in two parts)   Bark —2C **14**
Barkbythorpe Rd. Leic —1H **21**
Barker St. Leic —6F **21**
Barkford Clo. Leic —4E **23**
Barley Clo. Glen —5A **18**
Barley La. Count —6H **55**
Barmouth Av. Leic —3C **36**
Barnard Clo. Leic —2D **28**
Barnby Av. Wig —5E **37**
Barn Clo. Wig —3C **46**
Barnes Clo. Leic —6C **14**
Barnes Heath Rd. Lcic —2A **30**
Barnet Clo. Oad —6A **38**
Barnfield Clo. Gt G —2D **48**
Barngate Clo. Bir —3F **17**
Barnley Clo. Count —1E **55**
Barns Clo. Kir M —2C **24**
Barnsdale Rd. Leic —6H **11**
Barnstaple Clo. Wig —3B **46**
Barnstaple Rd. Leic —4D **30**
Barn Way. Mark —3C **8**
Barnwell Av. Leic —1B **20**
Baronet Way. Leic —4E **23**
Barons Clo. Kir M —2C **24**
Barratt Clo. Leic —5F **29**
Barrington Pk. Ind. Est. Leic
             —6B **12**
Barrington Rd. Leic —6G **29**
Barrow La. Glen —4H **17**
Barry Clo. Leic F —4E **25**
Barry Dri. Leic F —4E **25**
Barry Rd. Sys —5F **7**
Barry Rd. Leic —4D **22**
Barsby Wlk. Leic —1H **19**
  (in three parts)
Barshaw Pk. Ind. Est. Leic
             —6C **12**
Barston St. Leic —6B **20** (1C **4**)
Bartholomew St. Leic —3E **29**
Barton Clo. Rat —6D **16**
Barton Clo. Wig —2A **46**
Barton Rd. Leic —5F **29**
Barwell Rd. Kir M —2D **24**
Baslow Rd. Leic —3F **29**
Bassett Av. Count —2E **55**
Bassett La. Sap —6B **50**
Bassett St. Leic —6H **19**
Bassett St. Wig —2F **45**
Batchelor Rd. Flec —5B **58**
Bateman Rd. Leic —6E **19**
Bath Clo. Sap —5B **50**
Bath La. Leic —1A **28** (3A **4**)
Bath St. Leic —2C **20**
  (in two parts)
Bath St. Sys —5E **7**
Bathurst Rd. Leic —3D **30**
Battenberg Rd. Leic —1G **27**
Batten St. Leic —6A **28**
Battersbee Rd. Leic —5C **18**
Battersbee Wlk. Leic —5C **18**
Battersbee Way. Leic —5C **18**
Baxters Clo. Leic —2F **19**
Baycliff Clo. Leic —5F **19**

Bayham Clo. Leic —2B **30**
Baysdale. Wig —1D **46**
Bay St. Leic —6A **20** (1B **4**)
Bayswater Dri. Glen P —2D **44**
Beacon Av. Thurm —4D **14**
Beacon Clo. Glen —4B **18**
Beacon Clo. Grob —3E **17**
Beacon Clo. Leic —5A **12**
Beacon Clo. Mark —2C **8**
Beaconsfield Rd. Leic —3G **27**
Beadswell La. Bur O —3H **49**
Beal St. Leic —1D **28**
Beatrice Rd. Leic —6F **19**
Beatty Av. Leic —6G **21**
Beatty Rd. Leic —6G **21**
Beatty Rd. Sys —5F **7**
Beauchamp Rd. Kib —5H **59**
Beaufort Rd. Leic —6E **27**
Beaufort Way. Oad —5D **38**
Beaumanor Rd. Leic —3B **20**
Beaumont Grn. Grob —3F **17**
Beaumont Hall. Oad —1H **37**
Beaumont Leys Clo. Leic
             —2H **19**
Beaumont Leys La. Leic
             —6C **12**
Beaumont Leys Ter. Leic
             —1F **19**
Beaumont Lodge Rd. Leic
             —5B **12**
Beaumont Rd. Leic —1E **29**
Beaumont St. Oad —3A **38**
Beaumont Wlk. Leic —2E **19**
  (in two parts)
Beaumont Way. Leic —6A **12**
Beauville Dri. Leic —2E **19**
Beaver Cen., The. Leic —5B **28**
Beaver Clo. Glen P —6E **35**
Beck Clo. Glen P —6E **35**
Beckett Rd. Leic —5G **21**
Beckingham Rd. Leic —4E **29**
Bedale Dri. Leic —6C **12**
Bede St. Leic —2H **27**
Bedford Dri. Grob —3F **17**
Bedford Rd. Wig —6C **36**
Bedford St. N. Leic
          —6C **20** (1E **4**)
Bedford St. S. Leic
          —1B **28** (2D **4**)
Beeby Clo. Sys —6G **7**
Beeby Rd. Bark —3H **15**
Beeby Rd. Leic —1F **29**
Beeby Rd. Scrap —5F **23**
  (in two parts)
Beech Av. Grob —4E **17**
Beech Clo. Mark —3C **8**
Beech Ct. Wig —6F **37**
Beechcroft Av. Leic —1E **35**
Beechcroft Rd. Leic —6E **29**
Beech Dri. Leic —4B **26**
Beech Dri. Sys —1F **15**
Beechfield Av. Bir —4G **13**
Beechfield Clo. Gt G —2D **48**
Beechings Clo. Count —2D **54**
Beech Rd. Blab —4A **44**
Beech Rd. Oad —4A **38**
Beech St. Leic —6E **21**
Beech Tree Clo. Kib —3A **62**
Beech Wlk. Mark —3C **8**

Beechwood Av. Leic F —3G **25**
Beechwood Av. Quen —4H **7**
Beechwood Av. Thurm —5C **14**
Beechwood Clo. Leic —2C **30**
Beechwood Rd. L'thrpe —5D **42**
Beggar's La. Leic F & End
             —5E **25**
Begonia Clo. Leic F —5F **25**
Belfry Dri. Leic —2A **26**
Belgrave Av. Leic —2C **20**
Belgrave Boulevd. Leic —6C **12**
  (in two parts)
Belgrave Circ. Leic —5C **20**
Belgrave Flyover. Leic —6C **20**
Belgrave Ga. Leic
  (in two parts) —1B **28** (2D **4**)
Belgrave Ind. Cen. Leic —4C **20**
Belgrave Rd. Leic —5C **20**
Bellamy Clo. Glen P —6E **35**
Bell Clo. Rat —5C **16**
Belleville Dri. Oad —3C **38**
Belle Vue. Nar —3E **43**
Belle Vue Av. Leic —3A **20**
Bellflower Rd. Ham —2B **22**
Bellholme Clo. Leic —2D **20**
Bell La. Bur O —3H **49**
Bell La. Leic —1D **28**
Bell La. Nar —4E **43**
Bell St. Wig —6F **37**
Belmont St. Leic —2H **35**
Belper Clo. Oad —6A **38**
Belper Clo. Wig —3G **45**
Belper St. Leic —4D **20**
Belton Clo. Leic —4B **36**
Belton Rd. Leic —1E **35**
Belvoir Clo. Oad —5C **38**
Belvoir Dri. Leic —3G **35**
Belvoir Dri. Sys —5G **7**
Belvoir Dri. E. Leic —3H **35**
Belvoir St. Leic —2B **28** (5D **5**)
Beman Clo. Leic —6C **14**
Bembridge Clo. Leic —5H **19**
Bembridge Rd. Leic —5G **19**
Bencroft Clo. Ans —5F **11**
Bendbow Rise. Leic —4B **26**
  (in three parts)
Benford Clo. B Ast —3B **60**
Bennett Rise. Hunc —3A **42**
Bennetts Hill. Dun B —5F **61**
Bennetts La. Costn —1B **6**
Bennett Wlk. Leic —3D **26**
Bennett Way. Wig —2G **45**
Bennion Rd. Bush —3G **31**
Bennion Rd. Leic —2E **19**
Benscliffe Gdns. Leic —6H **35**
Benskins Oval. Leic —4C **12**
Benskin Wlk. Leic —3F **19**
Benskyn Clo. Count —1D **54**
Benson St. Leic —2G **29**
Bens Way. Leic —2B **30**
Bentburn Ho. Leic —6E **19**
Bentinghouse Gdns. Leic
             —5H **35**
Bentinghouse Rd. Leic —5H **35**
Bentley Rd. Bir —3G **13**
Beresford Dri. Leic —1F **37**
Berford Clo. B'Ast —2B **60**
Berkeley Clo. Oad —4D **38**
Berkenshaw Wlk. Leic —2B **30**

Berkley St. Leic —6A **20** (1B **4**)
Berkshire Rd. Leic —3H **35**
Berners St. Leic —1D **28**
Berridge Dri. Oad —4B **38**
Berridge La. Leic —2D **20**
Berridge St. Leic
          —2B **28** (4C **4**)
Berridge Wlk. Leic —2D **20**
Berrington Clo. Leic —5G **21**
Berry Ho. Wig —4B **46**
Berry's La. Rat —5C **16**
  (in two parts)
Best Clo. Wig —2F **45**
Beth-El. Wig —3A **46**
Bevan Rd. Leic —3C **12**
  (in two parts)
Beverley Av. Leic —4D **20**
Beverley Clo. Thurm —4C **14**
Beverley Dri. B Ast —6A **52**
Bevington Clo. Rat —4B **16**
Bewcastle Gro. Leic —6D **12**
Bewcastle Ho. Leic —6D **12**
Bewicke Rd. Leic —5F **27**
Bexhill Rise. Leic —6E **23**
Biam Way. Leic —1E **35**
Biddle Rd. Leic —6E **19**
Biddle Rd. L'thrpe —4E **43**
Biddulph Av. Leic —3E **29**
Biddulph St. Leic —3E **29**
Bideford Clo. Wig —4B **46**
Bideford Rd. Leic —4D **30**
Bidford Clo. Leic —5C **26**
Bidford Ct. Leic —5C **26**
Bidford Rd. Leic —5C **26**
Biggin Hill Rd. Leic —5B **30**
Biggs Clo. Whet —6A **44**
Bignall Dri. Leic F —3H **25**
Bilberry Clo. Leic —3E **35**
Billington Clo. Leic —2A **20**
Bilsdale Rd. Wig —2D **46**
Bindley La. Gt G —2D **48**
Bingley Clo. L'thrpe —5E **43**
Bingley Rd. L'thrpe —5E **43**
Birch Clo. Leic —4F **21**
Birchfield Av. Mark —3B **8**
Birch Tree Av. Bir —2G **13**
Birchtree Rd. Wig —5F **37**
Birchwood Clo. Leic F —5F **25**
Birdie Clo. Kib —5B **62**
Birds Nest Av. Leic —5D **18**
Birkdale Av. Leic —6F **29**
Birkdale Rd. Ans —5F **11**
Birkenshaw Rd. Leic —4E **19**
Birsmore Av. Leic —1F **21**
Birstall Rd. Bir —1C **20**
Birstall St. Leic —6D **20**
Birstow Cres. Leic —6D **12**
Bishopdale Rd. Leic —2G **19**
Bishopston Wlk. Leic —2B **20**
Bishop St. Leic —2B **28** (4D **4**)
Bisley St. Leic —4H **27**
Blaby By-Pass. Blab —4A **44**
Blaby Ind. Est. Blab —2A **44**
Blaby Rd. End —6H **33**
Blaby Rd. Wig —2F **45**
Blackberry La. Costn —1C **6**
Blackbird Av. Leic —5H **19**
Blackbird Rd. Leic —5H **19**
Blackett Av. Leic —5E **19**

Blackfriars St. Leic
　　　　　—1A **28** (3A **4**)
Blackmore Dri. Leic —2E **27**
Blacksmiths La. Sm W —6H **59**
Blackthorn Dri. Leic —5A **12**
Blackthorn Dri. Sys —5D **6**
Blackthorn La. Oad —2B **38**
Blackthorn Rd. Glen —6H **17**
(in two parts)
Blackwell Clo. Wig —2D **46**
Bladen Clo. Count —1D **54**
Blairmore Rd. Leic —1A **26**
Blaise Gro. Leic —4F **21**
Blake Ct. Nar —6G **33**
Blakenhall Clo. Nar —3B **42**
Blakenhall Rd. Leic —2A **30**
Blakesley Rd. Wig —6H **37**
Blakesley Wlk. Leic —3F **19**
(in two parts)
Blake St. Leic —1B **28** (2C **4**)
Blake Wlk. Leic —1B **28** (2C **4**)
Bland Rd. Leic —5D **18**
Blankley Dri. Leic —6F **29**
Blanklyn Av. Leic —2F **29**
Blaydon Clo. Leic —5F **19**
Blenheim Clo. Wig —3F **45**
Blenheim Cres. B Ast —6H **51**
Blenheim Rd. Bir —3H **13**
Blenheim Way. Leic —1A **20**
Blissett Rd. Leic —6E **19**
Bloomfield Rd. Leic —2B **36**
Blount Rd. Thurm —5D **14**
Bloxham Rd. Leic —6F **19**
Bloxoms Clo. Braun —3D **34**
Blue Banks Av. Glen P —6E **35**
Bluebell Clo. Kir M —1F **25**
Bluebell Clo. Quen —3H **7**
Bluebell Dri. Leic —5B **36**
Blue Gates Rd. Leic —6H **11**
Blue Pots Clo. Leic F —5F **25**
Blundell Rd. Leic —4A **30**
Blunt's La. Wig —1B **46**
Bodenham Clo. Wig —3A **46**
Bodicoat Clo. Whet —6A **44**
Bodkin Wlk. Leic —2F **19**
Bodmin Av. Wig —3A **46**
Bodnant Av. Leic —4G **29**
Bodycote Clo. B Ast —2B **60**
Bollington Rd. Oad —3C **38**
Bolsover St. Leic —1G **29**
Bolton Rd. Leic —2G **27**
Bonchurch St. Leic —6H **19**
Bondman Clo. Leic —1A **20**
Bonner Clo. Oad —5E **39**
Bonners La. Leic
　　　　　—3A **28** (6B **5**)
Bonney Rd. Leic —4E **19**
Bonnington Rd. Leic —6D **28**
Bonsall St. Leic —3E **29**
Bonville Pl. Leic —6F **27**
Booth Clo. Leic —2A **30**
Border Dri. Leic —6D **12**
Borlace St. Leic —1H **27**
Borrowcup Clo. Count —1C **54**
Borrowdale Way. Leic —4D **30**
Boston Rd. Leic —1D **18**
Boswell St. Nar —2C **42**
Bosworth Ho. Leic —5B **5**
Bosworth St. Leic —1G **27**

Botley Wlk. Leic —1A **30**
Boulder La. Leic —3B **36**
Boulevard Bldgs. Leic —5A **5**
Boulter Cres. Wig —6F **37**
Boulton Clo. B Ast —3B **60**
Boulton Ct. Oad —5E **39**
Boundary Rd. Leic —6H **27**
Bourne Mall. Leic —1E **19**
Bourton Cres. Oad —4C **38**
Bowhill Gro. Leic —1E **31**
Bowhill Way. Leic —6E **23**
Bowling Grn. St. Leic
　　　　　—2B **28** (4D **4**)
Bowmans Way. Glen —5H **17**
Bowmar's La. Leic
　　　　　—6A **20** (1A **4**)
Boyers Wlk. Leic F —4F **25**
Brabazon Rd. Oad —3H **37**
Bracken Clo. Leic —3B **30**
Bracken Clo. Leic F —5F **25**
Bracken Dale. E Gos —2H **7**
Brackenfield Way. Thurm
　　　　　—3E **15**
Bracken Hill. New L —4A **10**
Brackenthwaite. Leic —2F **21**
Bracken Wlk. Mark —2C **8**
Bracken Way. Mark —2C **8**
Brackley Clo. Leic —4G **21**
Bradbourne Rd. Leic —2F **29**
Bradbury Clo. Cosb —3F **53**
Bradfield Clo. Leic —2G **29**
Bradgate Av. Thurm —4D **14**
Bradgate Dri. Rat —4C **16**
Bradgate Dri. Wig —4D **36**
Bradgate Hill. Grob —6F **9**
Bradgate Mall. Leic —1F **19**
Bradgate Rd. Mark —2C **8**
Bradgate Rd. New L & Ans
　　　　　—3A **10**
Bradgate St. Leic —5H **19**
Brading Rd. Leic —5G **19**
Bradshaw Av. Glen P —6G **35**
Bradshaw Ct. Glen P —6G **35**
Bradston Rd. Leic —4A **36**
Braemar Clo. Leic —1E **21**
Braemar Dri. Leic —1E **21**
Brailsford Rd. Leic —2D **26**
Brailsford Rd. Wig —5D **36**
Bramall Ct. Leic —6G **21**
Bramall Rd. Leic —6G **21**
Bramber Clo. Thurm —5C **14**
Bramble Clo. Ham —3D **22**
Bramble Way. Leic —6E **27**
Brambling Rd. Leic —6F **21**
Brambling Way. Oad —4A **38**
Bramcote Clo. Leic —1F **35**
Bramcote Rd. Wig —6E **37**
Bramley Clo. B Ast —6A **52**
Bramley Ct. Glen —5H **17**
Bramley Orchard. Bush —2G **31**
Bramley Rd. Bir —4H **13**
Bramley Rd. Leic —1G **27**
Brampton Av. Leic —1F **27**
Brampton Way. Oad —3H **37**
Brancaster Clo. Leic —3H **19**
Brandon Ct. Blab —2B **44**
Brandon St. Leic —5C **20**
Bransdale Rd. Wig —1D **46**
Branting Hill Av. Glen —3H **17**

Branting Hill Gro. Glen —2H **17**
Brantin Hill. Grob —2H **17**
Bratmyr. Flec —4B **58**
Braunstone Av. Leic —5D **26**
(in two parts)
Braunstone Clo. Leic —6D **26**
Braunstone Frith Ind. Est. Leic F
(in three parts)　　—2H **25**
Braunstone Ga. Leic —2H **27**
Braunstone La. Leic —4A **26**
(in two parts)
Braunstone La. E. Leic —1F **35**
Braunstone Way. Leic —4C **26**
Braybrooke Rd. Leic —4G **21**
Braybrook Rd. Leic —4G **21**
Braymish Clo. Kib —5B **62**
Brazil St. Leic —4A **28**
Brecon Clo. Wig —1F **45**
Breedon Av. Wig —6E **37**
Breedon St. Leic —2E **29**
Brent Knowle Gdns. Leic
　　　　　—2D **30**
Brentwood Rd. Leic —6C **28**
Bretby Rd. Leic —3A **36**
Breton Clo. Kilb —2E **57**
Brettell Rd. Leic —5H **35**
Bretton Clo. Leic —2A **20**
Bretton Wlk. Leic —2A **20**
Brewer Clo. Leic —6C **14**
Brex Rise. Leic —1B **26**
Brian Rd. Leic —4H **19**
Brianway, The. Leic —6H **21**
Briar Clo. Oad —5B **38**
Briarfield Dri. Leic —4E **23**
Briargate Dri. Bir —3E **13**
Briar Meads. Oad —6A **38**
Briar Rd. Leic —6D **22**
Briar Wlk. Oad —5B **38**
Brickman Clo. Leic F —5E **25**
Bridevale Rd. Leic —4A **36**
Bridge Clo. Thurm —3D **14**
Bridge Pk. Rd. Thurm —4B **14**
Bridge Rd. Leic —1F **29**
Bridgewater Dri. Gt G —2C **48**
Bridgeway. Whet —4H **43**
Bridle Clo. Cft —2G **51**
Bridlespur Way. Leic —6E **13**
Bridle, The. Glen P —5F **35**
Bridport Clo. Wig —2B **46**
Brierfield Rd. Cosb —3F **53**
Brighton Av. Sys —5G **7**
Brighton Av. Wig —4E **37**
Brighton Rd. Leic —5F **21**
Brightside Rd. Leic —3G **29**
Bright St. Leic —6D **20**
Brightwell Dri. Leic F —3H **25**
Brindley Rise. Leic —4E **23**
Bringhurst Grn. Leic —6C **18**
Bringhurst Rd. Leic —6B **18**
Brington Clo. Wig —1C **46**
Brinsmead Rd. Leic —2D **36**
Bristol Av. Leic —4H **19**
Britannia St. Leic —6C **20**
Britannia Way. Thurm —2C **14**
Britford Av. Wig —3A **46**
Briton St. Leic —3H **27**
Brixham Dri. Leic —4C **36**
Brixworth Rise. Leic —1E **31**
Broad Av. Leic —2H **29**

Broadbent Clo. Whet —4H **43**
Broadfield Way. Count —1C **54**
Broadford Clo. Leic —1F **21**
Broadgate Clo. Bir —3G **13**
Broadhurst St. Leic —3D **20**
Broad Meadow. Wig —2C **46**
Broadmead Rd. Blab —5A **44**
Broad St. End —6H **33**
Broadway. Sys —6E **7**
Broadway Furlong. Ans —4G **11**
Broadway Rd. Leic —5F **29**
Broadway, The. Oad —6H **29**
Brockenhurst Dri. Leic —1C **34**
Brocklesby Way. Leic —5E **23**
Brocks Hill Clo. Oad —5B **38**
Brocks Hill Dri. Oad —4B **38**
Brodick Wlk. Leic —5F **21**
Bronze Barrow Clo. Wig
　　　　　—2D **46**
Brook Ct. Count —1F **55**
Brookdale Rd. Leic —2B **26**
Brookes Av. Cft —2G **51**
Brookes Ho. Cft —2G **51**
Brookfield Av. Sys —6F **7**
Brookfield Rise. Leic —3B **36**
Brookfield St. Sys —6F **7**
Brookfield Way. Kib —5B **62**
Brook Gdns. Glen P —6F **35**
Brookhouse Av. Leic —3D **28**
Brookhouse St. Leic —3D **28**
Brookland Rd. Leic —6C **28**
Brooklands Clo. B Ast —1B **60**
Brooklands Clo. Whet —4H **43**
Brooklands Rd. Cosb —1F **53**
Brook Rd. Leic —6D **22**
Brooksby Clo. Oad —3A **38**
Brooksby Dri. Oad —3A **38**
Brooksby St. Leic —6A **28**
Brookside. Bark —3H **15**
Brookside. Sys —5E **7**
(in two parts)
Brookside. Whet —5H **43**
Brookside Dri. Oad —4C **38**
Brook St. End —6H **33**
Brook St. Hunc —4H **41**
Brook St. Sys —5E **7**
Brook St. Thurm —4B **14**
Brook St. Whet —4H **43**
Broome La. E Gos —1G **7**
Broomfield. E Gos —2H **7**
Broomhills Rd. Nar —3B **42**
Broomleys. Count —1D **54**
Broom Way. Nar —2B **42**
Brougham St. Leic
　　　　　—1C **28** (2F **4**)
Broughton La. B Ast & Leir
　　　　　—3A **60**
Broughton Rd. Cosb —5D **52**
Broughton Rd. Cft —1G **51**
Broughton Rd. Leic —4A **36**
Broughton Rd. Sto S —3C **50**
Broughtons Field. Wig —3C **46**
Broughton Way. B Ast —5H **51**
Browning St. Leic —3G **27**
Browning St. Nar —2C **42**
Brown's Clo. Sap —5C **50**
Browns Way. Whet —6H **43**
Broxburn Clo. Leic —1F **21**

Broxfield Clo. Oad —6A **38**
Bruce St. Leic —4H **27**
Bruce Way. Whet —6G **43**
Bruin St. Leic —4C **20**
Bruins Wlk. Oad —4H **37**
Brunel Av. Leic —5E **19**
Brunswick St. Leic —1D **28**
Bruxby St. Sys —6D **6**
Bryngarth Cres. Leic —6B **22**
Bryony Rd. Ham —3D **22**
Buchan Wlk. Leic —2E **27**
Buckfast Clo. Leic —4H **29**
Buckfast Clo. Wig —2A **46**
Buckhaven Clo. Leic —1F **21**
Buckingham Clo. Grob —3E **17**
Buckingham Dri. Leic —4F **35**
Buckingham Rd. Count —1F **55**
Buckland Rd. Leic —5F **21**
Buckminster Rd. Leic —5G **19**
Bucksburn Wlk. Leic —1F **21**
Buckwell Rd. Sap —5B **50**
Bude Dri. Glen —4A **18**
Bude Rd. Wig —2B **46**
Buller Rd. Leic —4C **20**
Bull Head St. Wig —5F **37**
Bulwer Rd. Leic —6D **28**
(in two parts)
Burchnall Rd. Leic —6A **26**
Burdet Clo. Leic —6C **26**
Burfield St. Leic —5D **20**
Burgess Rd. Leic —3A **36**
Burgess St. Leic
—1A **28** (2B **4**)
Burgess St. Wig —6F **37**
Burgin Rd. Ans —6F **11**
Burleigh Av. Wig —5D **36**
Burley Clo. Cosb —2F **53**
Burleys Flyover. Leic
—6B **20** (1D **4**)
Burleys Way. Leic
—6B **20** (1C **4**)
Burlington Rd. Leic —6E **29**
Burnaby Av. Leic —1F **29**
Burnaston Rd. Leic —3A **36**
Burnell Rd. Leic —5F **27**
Burnet Clo. Ham —3C **22**
Burnham Clo. Leic —4B **46**
Burnham Ct. Cosb —3F **53**
Burnham Dri. Leic —3H **19**
Burnham Dri. Whet —5H **43**
Burnmoor St. Leic —5A **28**
Burnside Rd. B Ast —2B **60**
Burnside Rd. Leic —3C **36**
Burns St. Leic —1C **36**
Burns St. Nar —2D **42**
Burroughs Rd. Rat —5C **16**
Burrows, The. Nar —3B **42**
Bursdon Clo. Leic —1B **26**
Bursdon Ct. Leic —1B **26**
Bursom Ind. Est. Leic —5C **12**
Bursom Rd. Leic —5B **12**
Burton Clo. Oad —5D **38**
Burton St. Leic —1C **28** (3F **4**)
Buscot Clo. Leic —5F **21**
Bushby Rd. Leic —6F **21**
Bushey Clo. Nar —3D **42**
Bushloe Ct. Wig —1B **46**

Bushloe End. Wig —1A **46**
Bussett Rd. Leic —6F **19**
Butcombe Rd. Leic —4H **19**
Bute Way. Count —2F **55**
Butler Clo. Leic —1G **21**
Butt Clo. Wig —2C **46**
Butt Clo. La. Leic
—1B **28** (2C **4**)
Buttercup Clo. Nar —2C **42**
Buttermere St. Leic —4A **28**
Butterwick Dri. Leic —1G **19**
Buxton Clo. Whet —4A **44**
Buxton St. Leic —1E **29**
Byfield Dri. Wig —6G **37**
Byford Rd. Leic —3A **20**
Byre Cres. B Ast —2B **60**
Byron Clo. Flec —6C **58**
Byron Clo. Nar —1C **42**
Byron Ct. Flec —6B **58**
Byron St. Leic —1C **28** (2E **4**)
Byway Rd. Leic —5G **29**

Cademan Clo. Leic —2D **36**
Cadle Clo. Sto S —2B **50**
Cairngorm Clo. Leic —2B **36**
Cairnsford Rd. Leic —3D **36**
Calais Hill. Leic —2C **28** (5E **5**)
Calais St. Leic —2C **28** (5E **5**)
Caldecott Clo. Wig —1C **46**
Caldecott Rd. Leic —6E **27**
Calder Ho. Leic —6G **35**
Calder Rd. Leic —2G **19**
Caledine Rd. Leic —5E **19**
Calgary Rd. Leic —6C **20**
Callan Clo. Nar —3C **42**
Calver Hey Rd. Leic —2E **19**
Calvert Cres. Sap —6C **50**
Calverton Av. Wig —5E **37**
Calverton Clo. Rat —5C **16**
Camborne Clo. Wig —2A **46**
Cambrian Clo. Cosb —3F **53**
Cambridge Rd. Cosb & & LE8
—2F **53**
Cambridge St. Leic —3G **27**
Camden Rd. Leic —6E **27**
Camden St. Leic —1C **28** (3E **4**)
Camellia Clo. Nar —2B **42**
Camelot Way. Nar —2C **42**
Cameron Av. Leic —2D **20**
Camfield Rise. Leic —5H **35**
Campbell Av. Thurm —5C **14**
Campbell St. Leic
—2C **28** (5F **5**)
Campion Clo. Nar —3C **42**
Campion Wlk. Leic —2E **19**
Camville Rd. Leic —3D **26**
Canal St. Leic —2G **35**
Canal St. Thurm —3B **14**
Canal St. Wig —3F **45**
Cank St. Leic —2B **28** (4C **4**)
Cannam Clo. Whet —6A **44**
Canning Pl. Leic —6B **20** (1C **4**)
Canning St. Leic —6B **20** (1C **4**)
Cannock St. Leic —1A **22**
Canon Clo. Oad —4B **38**
Canons Clo. Nar —3D **42**
Canonsleigh Rd. Leic —2A **20**
Canonsleigh Wlk. Leic —2A **20**

Canon St. Leic —3D **20**
Canterbury Ter. Leic —4F **27**
Cantrell Rd. Leic —4B **26**
Canvey Clo. Wig —6H **37**
Capers Clo. End —6G **33**
Capesthorne Clo. Leic —5G **21**
Captains La. Mark —3B **8**
Carberry Clo. Oad —5D **38**
Cardigan Dri. Wig —1F **45**
Cardinal Clo. Rat —5C **16**
Cardinals Wlk. Leic —5C **22**
Carey Clo. Wig —3B **46**
Carey Hill Rd. Sto S —3B **50**
Carey Rd. Hunc —4H **41**
Carey's Clo. Leic
—2A **28** (4B **4**)
Carfax Av. Oad —2H **37**
Carisbrooke Av. Leic —2E **37**
Carisbrooke Gdns. Leic —1E **37**
Carisbrooke Pk. Leic —2E **37**
Carisbrooke Rd. Leic —1E **37**
Carlisle St. Leic —2F **27**
Carl St. Leic —3G **35**
Carlton Av. Nar —3E **43**
Carlton Dri. Wig —6E **37**
Carlton La. Bur O —3H **49**
Carlton Rd. Kib —3A **62**
Carlton St. Leic —3B **28** (6C **5**)
Carmen Gro. Grob —2D **16**
Carnation Clo. Leic F —5F **25**
Carnation St. Leic —3B **20**
Carnoustie Rd. Leic —2B **26**
Caroline Ct. Leic —3A **36**
Carpenters Clo. Glen —6H **17**
Carpe Rd. Leic —4F **21**
Carrow Rd. Leic —2H **25**
Carter Clo. End —6G **33**
Carter St. Leic —5E **21**
Carts La. Leic —1B **28** (3C **4**)
Cartwright Dri. Oad —4H **37**
Cashmore View. Leic —1H **19**
Castell Dri. Grob —2F **17**
Castle Clo. Sap —6B **50**
Castle Fields. Leic —6A **12**
Castleford Rd. Leic —1C **34**
Castlegate Av. Bir —3F **13**
Castle Rise. Grob —3F **17**
Castle Rd. Kir M —2D **24**
Castle St. Leic —2A **28** (4B **4**)
Castleton Rd. Wig —5E **37**
Castle View. Leic —2A **28** (5B **5**)
Caswell Clo. Leic —1H **19**
Caters Clo. Ans —5F **11**
Catesby St. Leic —2H **27**
Catherine St. Leic —6D **20**
Catherine St. Ind. Est. Leic
—3F **21**
Cathkin Clo. Leic —2B **26**
Caudle Clo. Crop —1H **11**
Causeway La. Crop —1G **11**
Causeway La. Leic
—1A **28** (2B **4**)
Cavendish Rd. Leic —6A **28**
Caversham Rd. Leic —6G **35**
Cawsand Rd. Wig —2A **46**
Cecil Gdns. Leic —1E **29**
Cecilia Rd. Leic —5D **28**
Cecil Rd. Leic —1D **28**
Cedar Av. Bir —4G **13**

Cedar Av. Wig —1B **46**
Cedar Clo. Glen —4C **18**
Cedar Clo. Kib —5H **59**
Cedar Ct. Grob —3F **17**
Cedar Cres. Nar —4D **42**
Cedar Dri. Sys —1F **15**
Cedar Rd. Blab —5B **44**
Cedar Rd. Leic —3E **29**
Cedars Ct. Leic —5E **29**
Cedars, The. Leic —2D **36**
Cedarwood Clo. Leic —4F **21**
Celadine Rd. Leic —3C **22**
Celt St. Leic —3H **27**
Cemetery Rd. Whet —4H **43**
Central Av. Leic —5E **29**
Central Av. Sys —5F **7**
Central Av. Wig —1H **45**
Central Clo. Whet —3H **43**
Central Rd. Leic —6H **19**
Central St. Count —1F **55**
Centre Ct. Leic —2B **34**
Centurion Ct. Rat —6D **16**
Centurion Way. Leic —1B **34**
Chadderton Clo. Leic —2C **36**
Chadwell Rd. Leic —6C **18**
Chadwick Wlk. Leic —2H **19**
Chaffinch Clo. Leic —5B **12**
Chainama Clo. Leic —1A **26**
Chale Rd. Leic —3D **20**
Chalgrove Wlk. Leic —1A **30**
Chalvington Clo. Leic —4C **30**
Chambers Clo. Mark —3D **8**
Champion Clo. Leic —2B **30**
Chancel Rd. Leic —3C **12**
Chancery St. Leic
—2B **28** (5C **5**)
Chandler Way. B Ast —2D **60**
Chandos St. Leic —3E **29**
Chantry Clo. Hunc —4H **41**
Chapel Clo. Sys —5E **7**
Chapel Clo. Thurc —1B **12**
Chapel Grn. Leic F —4H **25**
Chapel Hill. Grob —2E **17**
Chapel La. Cosb —3F **53**
Chapel La. Leic —1D **36**
Chapel La. Rat —5C **16**
Chapel La. Wig —1B **46**
Chapel St. Blab —2B **44**
Chapel St. End —6G **33**
Chapel St. Oad —4A **38**
Chapel St. Sys —5E **7**
Chappell Clo. Thurm —4C **14**
Charlecote Av. Leic —6D **26**
Charles Dri. Ans —5G **11**
Charles St. Leic —1B **28** (2D **4**)
Charles Way. Oad —4C **38**
Charles Way. Whet —6A **44**
Charlotte Clo. Blab —3A **44**
Charlton Clo. Whet —5A **44**
Charnor Rd. Leic —6C **18**
Charnwood. Rat —4B **16**
Charnwood Av. Thurm —3D **14**
Charnwood Av. Whet —3H **43**
Charnwood Clo. Leic F —3G **25**
Charnwood Dri. Leic F —4G **25**
Charnwood Dri. Mark —3D **8**
Charnwood Dri. Thurm —2F **15**
Charnwood Rd. Ans —4F **11**

Charnwood St. Leic —1E **29**
Charnwood Wlk. Leic —6E **21**
Charter St. Leic —6B **20**
Chartley Rd. Leic —4G **27**
Chartwell Dri. Wig —6C **36**
Chartwell Trading Est. Wig
—6C **36**
Chase, The. E Gos —1H **7**
Chase, The. Gt G —2E **49**
Chase, The. Leic —2D **34**
Chase, The. Mark —3C **8**
Chater Clo. Leic —6D **22**
Chatham St. Leic
—2B **28** (5D **5**)
Chatsworth Av. Wig —2G **45**
Chatsworth Dri. Sys —6D **6**
Chatsworth St. Leic —6C **28**
Chatteris Av. Leic —4D **30**
Chaucer St. Leic —4E **29**
Chaucer St. Nar —2C **42**
Cheapside. Leic —1B **28** (3C **4**)
Checketts Clo. Leic —3D **20**
Checketts Rd. Leic —2C **20**
Checkland Rd. Thurm —3C **14**
Cheddar Rd. Wig —6G **37**
Cheer Clo. Whet —1H **53**
Chellaston Rd. Wig —5E **37**
Chelsea Clo. Glen P —2D **44**
Cheltenham Rd. Leic —3G **19**
Cheney Ct. Hunc —4H **41**
Cheney End. Hunc —4H **41**
Chepstow Rd. Leic —4E **29**
Cheriton Rd. Leic —4H **35**
Cherrybrook Clo. Leic —4B **12**
Cherry Dri. Sys —1F **15**
Cherry Gro. Gt G —2E **49**
Cherryleas Dri. Leic —3G **27**
Cherry Rd. Blab —4B **44**
Cherry St. Wig —1H **45**
Cherry Tree Av. Leic F —4E **25**
Cherrytree Clo. Ans —6F **11**
Cherry Tree Clo. Count —1E **55**
Cherry Tree Ct. Leic F —4E **25**
Cherry Tree Gro. End —6G **33**
Cheshire Dri. Wig —6C **36**
Cheshire Gdns. Leic —2H **35**
Cheshire Rd. Leic —2H **35**
Chester Clo. Blab —4C **44**
Chester Clo. Leic —6D **20**
Chesterfield Rd. Leic —3F **29**
Chester Rd. Blab —4C **44**
Chesterton Ct. Nar —1C **42**
Chesterton Wlk. Leic —2E **27**
(off Gaskell Wlk.)
Chestnut Av. Leic —4C **22**
Chestnut Av. Oad —4H **37**
Chestnut Clo. B Ast —2C **60**
Chestnut Clo. L'thrpe —5D **42**
Chestnut Clo. Quen —4H **7**
Chestnut Clo. Sys —1F **15**
Chestnut Dri. Bush —5D **52**
Chestnut Grange. B Ast —2B **60**
Chestnut Rd. Glen —5A **18**
Chestnuts, The. Count —1E **55**
Chestnut Wlk. Grob —3F **17**
Chettle Rd. Leic —6E **19**
Chevin Av. Leic —2B **26**
Cheviot Rd. Leic —3B **36**
Chilcombe Clo. Leic —2A **20**

Chilcombe Wlk. Leic —2A **20**
Chiltern Av. Cosb —3F **53**
Chiltern Grn. Leic —3C **36**
Chiswick Rd. Leic —6B **28**
Chitterman Way. Mark —3C **8**
Chorley Wood Rd. Leic —3D **30**
Chrisett Clo. Leic —1B **30**
Christopher Clo. Count —2E **55**
Christopher Dri. Leic —1H **21**
Christow St. Leic
—6C **20** (1F **4**)
Church Av. Leic —2G **27**
Church Clo. B Ast —1B **60**
Church Clo. Dun B —5F **61**
Church Clo. Kib —4A **62**
Church Dri. Mark —3B **8**
Church Ga. Leic —1B **28** (2C **4**)
Church Hill. Bir —5H **13**
Church Hill. Scrap —5F **23**
Church Hill Rd. Thurm —4C **14**
Churchill Clo. Oad —4A **38**
Churchill Dri. Leic F —3H **25**
Churchill St. Leic —3D **28**
Churchill Way. Flec —6C **58**
Church La. Ans —5F **11**
Church La. Dun B —6F **61**
Church La. Flec —6B **58**
Church La. Leic —2D **36**
Church La. Nar —3E **43**
Church La. Rat —5C **16**
Church La. Stoug —6E **31**
Church La. Thurm —4C **14**
Church La. Thurn —3F **31**
Church La. Whet —3H **43**
Church Nook. Wig —6F **37**
Church Rd. Ayl —3G **35**
Church Rd. Belg —2C **20**
Church Rd. Evi —5B **30**
Church Rd. Glen —4H **17**
Church Rd. Gt G —3C **48**
Church Rd. Kib —5A **62**
Church Rd. Kir M —2D **24**
Church Rd. Wan —1A **14**
Church St. Blab —3B **44**
Church St. Count —2F **55**
Church St. Leic —2C **28** (4E **4**)
Church St. Oad —4A **38**
Church St. Sap —6B **50**
Church St. Sto S —3C **50**
Church St. Thurl —6A **32**
Church St. Thurm —5B **14**
Church View. Nar —3E **43**
Church Wlk. Blab —3B **44**
Church Wlk. Leic —2C **20**
Church Wlk. Sap —6B **50**
Churchward Av. Leic —1G **19**
Circle, The. Leic —2H **29**
City, The. Kib —3A **62**
Clarefield Rd. Leic —2F **27**
Clare Gro. Braun —5B **26**
Claremont St. Leic —2C **20**
Clarence Rd. Nar —1F **43**
Clarence St. Leic —1B **28** (2D **4**)
Clarendon Pk. Rd. Leic —6C **28**
Clarendon St. Leic
—3A **28** (7B **5**)
Clarke Gro. Bir —5G **13**
Clarkes Rd. Wig —1H **45**
Clarke St. Leic —2D **20**

Clark Gdns. Blab —3A **44**
Claybrook Av. Leic —1E **35**
Claydon Rd. Leic —5G **21**
Claymill Rd. Leic —1H **21**
Clayton Dri. Thurm —5D **14**
Clematis Clo. Leic —6A **12**
Clement Av. Leic —2C **20**
Clephan Building. Leic —5B **5**
Clevedon Cres. Leic —5G **21**
Cleveland Rd. Wig —5F **37**
Cleveleys Av. Leic —1E **35**
Cliffe La. Mark —2A **8**
Cliffe Rd. Bir —5F **13**
Clifford St. Leic —1H **27**
Clifford St. Wig —2F **45**
Cliffwood Av. Bir —4F **13**
Clifton Dri. Wig —3G **45**
Clifton Rd. Leic —1A **36**
Clint Hill Dri. Sto S —2C **50**
Clipper Rd. Leic —2H **21**
Clipstone Clo. Wig —1C **46**
Clipstone Gdns. Wig —1C **46**
Clipstone Ho. Leic —2D **28**
Clipstone St. Leic —2D **28**
Close, The. Ans —4F **11**
Close, The. Blab —2B **44**
Close, The. Leic —1C **42**
Close, The. Rat —4C **16**
Clovelly Rd. Glen —5B **18**
Clovelly Rd. Leic —3H **29**
Clover Clo. Nar —3C **42**
Clover Wlk. E Gos —2H **7**
Clumber Clo. Sys —4F **7**
Clumber Rd. Leic —2G **29**
Clyde St. Leic —1C **28** (2F **4**)
Coalbourn Clo. Leic —1A **20**
Coales Av. Whet —6A **44**
Coatbridge Av. Leic —1F **21**
Coates Av. Leic —6E **19**
Cobbett Rd. Braun —5B **26**
Cobden St. Leic —5D **20**
Cobden St. Ind. Est. Leic
—6E **21**
Codwells Clo. Flec —6C **58**
Cokayne Rd. Leic —1B **26**
Colbert Dri. Leic —2E **35**
Colbrook Wlk. Leic —4G **29**
Colby Dri. Thurm —6D **14**
Colby Rd. Thurm —6D **14**
Colchester Rd. Leic —1B **30**
Colebrook Clo. Leic —4G **29**
Coleford Rd. Leic —6E **15**
Coleman Clo. Leic —6H **21**
Coleman Rd. Flec —5B **58**
Coleman Rd. Leic —6H **21**
Coleridge Dri. Nar —1C **42**
Coles Clo. Leic —6B **14**
Colindale Av. Bir —3G **13**
Colin Grundy Dri. Leic —4B **22**
Collaton Rd. Wig —1A **46**
College Av. Leic —3D **28**
College Hall. Leic —1E **37**
College Rd. Sys —1F **15**
College Rd. Whet —3H **43**
College St. Leic —3D **28**
Collett Rd. Leic —1G **19**
Collingham Rd. Leic —5G **27**
Collin Pl. Leic —3E **21**
Collins Clo. Braun —5B **26**

Colne Clo. Oad —4D **38**
Colsterdale Clo. Leic —6D **12**
Coltbeck Av. Nar —3C **42**
Colthurst Way. Leic —1E **31**
Colton St. Leic —2C **28** (4E **4**)
Coltsford Rd. Leic —3C **22**
Columbia Clo. End —6G **33**
Columbine Clo. Leic —5C **26**
Columbine Rd. Ham —2B **22**
Colwell Rd. Leic —5H **19**
Combe Clo. Leic —5G **19**
Comet Clo. Leic —6F **19**
Commercial Sq. Leic —5B **28**
Common, The. Evi —4A **30**
Compass Rd. Leic —6D **22**
(in three parts)
Compton Dri. Hunc —3H **41**
Compton Rd. Leic —5G **27**
Conaglen Rd. Leic —3F **35**
Condor Clo. B Ast —6B **52**
Conduit St. Leic —2C **28** (5F **5**)
Cone La. Leic —5E **29**
Conery La. End —5G **33**
Coneygrey. Flec —4B **58**
Conifer Clo. Leic —3E **29**
Conifers Caravan Pk. Rat
—6D **16**
Coningsby Clo. Leic —6F **27**
Coniston Av. Leic —4A **28**
Coniston Way. Cft —1H **51**
Connaught St. Leic —3D **28**
Constable Av. Leic —5D **20**
Constance Rd. Leic —2F **29**
Constitution Hill. Leic
—2C **28** (4F **4**)
Conway Rd. Leic —4F **29**
Cooden Av. Leic —3F **27**
Cooke Clo. Braun —5B **26**
Cooke's Dri. B Ast —1A **60**
Cooks La. Sap —6B **50**
Cooks La. Wig —3C **46**
Cooks Wlk. Glen —5A **18**
Coombe Pl. Oad —5B **38**
Coombe Rise. Oad —5C **38**
Co-operation St. End —6H **33**
Cooper Clo. Hunc —3A **42**
Cooper Clo. Leic —3G **35**
Cooper Gdns. Oad —5D **38**
Cooper's La. Dun B —5F **61**
Cooper's Nook. E Gos —2H **7**
Cooper St. Leic —4C **20**
Copdale Rd. Leic —2G **29**
Copeland Av. Leic —4E **19**
Copeland Rd. Bir —5F **13**
Copinger Rd. Leic —2B **36**
Coplow Av. Leic —5G **29**
Coplow Cres. Sys —1E **15**
Coppice, The. Count —1E **55**
Coppice, The. Mark —3C **8**
Coppice, The. Nar —3C **42**
Coppice, The. Oad —1H **37**
Coppice, The. Thurm —4E **15**
Copse Clo. Leic F —6F **25**
Copse Clo. Oad —2C **38**
Copthorne Clo. Leic —2B **26**
Copt Oak Ct. Nar —3C **42**
Copt Oak Rd. Nar —3C **42**
Corah St. Leic —2A **28** (5A **5**)
Coral St. Leic —4C **20**

Corbet Clo. Leic —2F **19**
Cordelia Clo. Leic —4G **21**
Cordery Rd. Leic —3B **30**
Corfield Rise. Leic —4C **26**
Cork La. Glen P —1A **44**
(in two parts)
Cork St. Leic —2E **29**
Cornfield Clo. L'thrpe —4E **43**
Cornwallis Av. Leic —3F **19**
Cornwall Rd. Leic —4H **19**
Cornwall Rd. Wig —1F **45**
Cornwall St. End —6H **33**
Coronation Av. D Ast —1A **60**
Coronation Av. Wig —1H **45**
Corporation Rd. Leic —3B **20**
Corshaw Wlk. Leic —5F **21**
Cort Cres. Leic —3C **26**
Cosby Hill. Cosb —1H **61**
Cosby La. Cosb —1H **61**
Cosby Rd. B Ast —1B **60**
Cosby Rd. Count —2B **54**
Cosby Rd. L'thrpe —5E **43**
Cossington La. Costn —2D **6**
Cossington Rd. Sile —1A **6**
Cossington St. Leic —4D **20**
Coteman Ct. Leic —6H **21**
Cotley Rd. Leic —6C **12**
Cotman Wlk. Leic —5D **20**
Cotswold Av. Cosb —2G **53**
Cotswold Grn. Leic — 6C **12**
Cottage Clo. Rat —4C **16**
Cottage Farm Clo. Braun
—3D **34**
Cottage La. B Ast —1C **60**
Cottage La. Ind. Est. B Ast
—1C **60**
Cottage Rd. Wig —2C **46**
Cottage Row. Leic —1F **35**
Cottagers Clo. Leic —4A **36**
Cottesbrook Clo. Wig —1B **46**
Cottesmore Av. Oad —5D **38**
Cottesmore Rd. Leic —6F **21**
Cotton Clo. B Ast —2B **60**
Cotton Clo. Leic —6B **14**
Coulson Clo. Whet —5A **44**
Countesthorpe Rd. Cosb &
(in two parts)   Count —3F **53**
Countesthorpe Rd. Whet
—4C **44**
Countesthorpe Rd. Wig —2F **45**
(in two parts)
Countryman's Way. E Gos
—1H **7**
Countryman Way. Mark —3C **8**
Court Clo. Kir M —2E **25**
Courtenay Rd. Leic —4G **19**
Court Rd. Glen P —1B **44**
Court Rd. Thurn —3F **31**
Coventry Rd. B Ast —5G **51**
Coventry Rd. Sap & Cft —6E **51**
Coventry St. Leic —2H **27**
Coverack Clo. Leic —3H **29**
Coverdale Rd. Wig —2D **46**
Coverside Rd. Gt G —2D **48**
Covert Clo. Oad —5D **38**
Covert Clo. Sys —5C **6**
Covert La. Scrap —6F **23**
Covert, The. E Gos —1H **7**
Covett Way. Leic —2C **26**

Cowdall Rd. Leic —3C **26**
Cowley Way. Leic —6E **23**
Cowslip Clo. Nar —3B **42**
Crabtree Corner. Leic —4C **36**
Cradock Rd. Leic —5D **28**
Cradock St. Leic —1D **28**
Crafton St. E. Leic
—1C **28** (2F **4**)
Crafton St. W. Leic
—1C **28** (2E **4**)
Craig Gdns. Leic —1B **26**
Craighill Rd. Leic —1D **36**
Craighill Wlk. Leic —1D **36**
Cranberry Clo. Leic —5B **26**
Cranborne Gdns. Oad —1B **38**
(in three parts)
Cranbrook Rd. Thurn —1F **31**
Crane Ley Rd. Grob —2E **17**
Cranesbill Rd. Leic —4C **22**
Crane St. Leic —6B **20** (1C **4**)
Cranfield Rd. Leic —3H **35**
Cranmer Clo. Blab —5A **44**
Cranmer Dri. Sys —6D **6**
Cranmer St. Leic —3H **27**
Cranston Cres. Glen —6A **18**
Crantock Clo. Leic —4D **30**
Cranwell Clo. Leic —5B **30**
Craven St. Leic —6A **20** (1B **4**)
Crayburn Ho. Leic —5E **19**
Crayford Way. Leic —4D **22**
Craythorne Way. Wig —1D **46**
Creaton Ct. Wig —1C **46**
Creaton Rd. Wig —1C **46**
Crediton Clo. Wig —3B **46**
Crescent St. Leic
—3B **28** (6D **5**)
Crescent, The. Blab —4B **44**
Crescent, The. Leic
—3B **28** (6D **5**)
Crescent, The. Wig —5E **37**
Cressida Pl. Leic —5C **26**
Cresswell Clo. Thurm —5E **15**
Crestway, The. Whet —3H **43**
Crete Av. Wig —1E **45**
Crislehurst Av. Leic —1C **34**
Critchlow Rd. Hunc —3H **41**
Croft Av. Leic —3G **35**
Croft Dri. Wig —4D **36**
Crofters Clo. Glen —5G **17**
Crofters Dri. Leic —6A **22**
Croft Hill Rd. Hunc —5G **41**
Croft Rd. Cosb —1B **52**
Croft Rd. Leic —4C **12**
Croft Rd. Thurl —2E **41**
Crofts, The. Mark —2B **8**
Croft, The. Kir M —2E **25**
Croft Way. B Ast —1C **60**
Croft Way. Mark —3B **8**
Cromarty Clo. Leic —2F **21**
Cromer St. Leic —4E **29**
Cromford Av. Wig —2G **45**
Cromford Rd. Cosb —1F **53**
Cromford St. Leic —1E **29**
Cromford Way. B Ast —1D **60**
Cromwell Ho. Leic —1B **36**
Cromwell Rd. Gt G —3D **48**
Cropston Rd. Crop —1G **11**
Cropthorne Av. Leic —2H **29**
Cross Farm Ct. Sto S —3C **50**

Cross Hedge Clo. Leic —1G **19**
Cross Keys Grn. Leic —6E **23**
Crossleys. Flec —6B **58**
Crossley St. Glen —5A **18**
Cross Rd. Leic —5E **29**
Cross St. Blab —3B **44**
Cross St. End —6H **33**
Cross St. Leic —4C **20**
Cross St. Oad —2A **38**
Cross St. Sys —6F **7**
Cross St. Wig —1B **46**
Cross, The. End —6H **33**
Cross Wlk. Leic —1A **30**
Crossways, The. —4G **13**
Crossways, The. Leic —3B **36**
Crossway, The. Braun —1E **35**
Crowan Dri. Wig —2A **46**
Crowfoot Way. B Ast —3B **60**
Crowhurst Dri. Leic —1C **34**
Crow La. Leic —4H **27**
Crown Hills Av. Leic —2G **29**
Crown Hills Rise. Leic —2G **29**
Croyde Clo. Leic —3H **29**
Croyland Grn. Leic —1E **31**
Cufflin Clo. Rat —5D **16**
Cuffling Clo. Leic —2B **26**
Cuffling Dri. Leic —1B **26**
Culham Av. Leic —5F **21**
Culver Rd. Leic —5G **19**
Culworth Dri. Wig —1C **46**
Cumberland Rd. Wig —6A **36**
Cumberland St. Leic
—1A **28** (2B **4**)
Cumberwell Dri. Nar —2F **43**
Curlew Clo. Sys —5C **6**
Curlew Wlk. Leic —6E **21**
Curtis Clo. Whet —4A **44**
Curtleys Clo. Leic —6F **27**
Curzon Av. Bir —5G **13**
Curzon Av. Wig —2G **45**
Curzon La: Quen —4H **7**
Curzon Rd. Leic —2A **36**
Curzon St. Leic —6D **20**
Cutters Clo. Nar —4D **42**
Cuttings, The. Thurn —1F **31**
Cygnet Clo. Sys —5D **6**
Cyprus Rd. Leic —3A **36**
Cyril St. Leic —1E **35**

Dabey Dri. Mark —3B **8**
Dakyn Rd. Leic —1D **30**
Dalby Av. Bir —3H **13**
Dalby Av. Bush —2G **31**
Dalby Dri. Grob —2F **17**
Dalby Rd. Ans —4F **11**
Dale Acre. Count —1F **55**
Dale Av. Wig —5C **36**
Dales, The. Count —1C **54**
Dale St. Leic —2E **29**
Dalketh Rd. Leic —1F **21**
Dalley Clo. Sys —1F **15**
Danbury Dri. Leic —4H **19**
Dandees Clo. Mark —2C **8**
Danehill. Rat —4C **16**
Danehurst Av. Leic —1F **27**
Danes Hill Rd. Leic —2G **27**
Dane St. Leic —2H **27**
Dannett St. Leic —1H **27**

Dannett Wlk. Leic —2H **27**
Danvers Rd. Leic —4G **27**
Darenth Dri. Leic —2E **19**
Darker St. Leic —1B **28** (2C **4**)
Darley Av. Wig —2G **45**
Darley Rd. Blab —4A **44**
Darley St. Leic —2E **29**
Darlington Rd. Leic —5E **19**
Dart Clo. Oad —4D **38**
Dartford Rd. Leic —6H **27**
Darwen Clo. Leic —5F **19**
Darwin Clo. B Ast —2B **60**
Dashwood Rd. Leic —4E **29**
Davenport Av. Oad —4H **37**
Davenport Rd. Leic —2B **30**
Davenport Rd. Wig —2A **46**
Davett Clo. Leic —1B **30**
David Av. Leic —6E **13**
Davison Clo. Leic —1A **30**
Dawlish Clo. Leic —2D **30**
Daybell Clo. Whet —2H **43**
Day St. Leic —2C **20**
Deacon Rd. Leic —3C **12**
Deacon St. Leic —3A **28** (6B **5**)
Deancourt Rd. Leic —3D **36**
Deanery Cres. Leic —3D **12**
Dean Rd. Leic —4E **21**
Deansburn Ho. Leic —5D **18**
Deepdale. Leic —1H **29**
Delaware Rd. Leic —3E **31**
Demontfort Ct. Ans —5F **11**
De Montfort Ho. Leic
—3B **28** (6C **5**)
De Montfort M. Leic
—3C **28** (6F **5**)
De Montfort Pl. Leic
—3C **28** (6F **5**)
De Montfort Sq. Leic
—3C **28** (7E **5**)
De Montfort St. Leic
—4C **28** (8E **5**)
Denacre Av. Wig —2G **45**
Denbydale. Wig —2D **46**
Denegate Av. Bir —3F **13**
Denham Clo. Leic —1A **26**
Denis Clo. Leic —1F **27**
Deniston Clo. B Ast —6H **51**
Denman La. Hunc —3H **41**
Denmark Rd. Leic —1A **36**
Denmead Av. Wig —5E **37**
Dennison Vs. Flec —6B **58**
Denton St. Leic —2F **27**
Denton Wlk. Wig —1C **46**
Derby Clo. B Ast —2C **60**
Derry Wlk. Leic —1A **20**
Dersingham Rd. Leic —3H **19**
Derwent St. Leic —2E **29**
Derwent Wlk. Oad —4C **38**
Desford La. Kir M —1A **24**
Desford Rd. Des & End —1B **32**
Desford Rd. Kir M —1D **24**
Desford Rd. Nar —3D **42**
Desford Rd. Thurl —5A **32**
Devana Rd. Leic —4E **29**
Devitt Way. B Ast —3B **60**
(in two parts)
Devonia Rd. Oad —5E **39**
Devonshire Av. Wig —2G **45**
Devonshire Ct. Oad —5B **38**

Devonshire Rd. Leic —4A **20**
Devonshire St. Leic
　　　　　—6B **20** (1C **4**)
Devonshire Wlk. Oad —6C **38**
Devon Way. Leic —2H **29**
Dickens Ct. Leic —2E **27**
Dicken, The. Whet —4H **43**
Dickinson Way. Thurm —4D **14**
Didsbury St. Leic —3C **26**
Digby Clo. Leic —4F **27**
Digby Ho. Oad —2H **37**
Dillon Grn. Leic —4D **18**
Dillon Rise. Leic —5D **18**
Dillon Rd. Leic —5D **18**
Dillon Way. Leic —4D **18**
Dimmingsdale Clo. Ans —4G **11**
Dingley Av. Leic —4E **21**
Dingly Link. Wig —6H **37**
Diseworth St. Leic —2E **29**
Disney Clo. Sto S —3B **50**
Disraeli Clo. Kib —5H **59**
Disraeli St. Leic —2G **35**
Ditchling Av. Leic —1E **27**
Dixon Dri. Leic —4E **29**
Dobney Av. Quen —3G **7**
Dog and Gun La. Whet —6H **43**
Dollier St. Kib —5H **59**
Dolphin Sq. Leic —4D **4**
Dominion Rd. Glen —5A **18**
Donald Clo. Leic —1H **21**
Donaldson Rd. Leic —5C **20**
Doncaster Rd. Leic —4D **20**
Donnett Clo. Leic —1B **30**
Donnington St. Leic —2E **29**
Dorchester Clo. Blab —5C **44**
Dorchester Clo. Wig —3B **46**
Dorchester Rd. Leic —3F **27**
Dore Rd. Leic —3E **29**
Dorothy Av. Glen P —6F **35**
Dorothy Av. Thurm —5B **14**
Dorothy Rd. Leic —2F **29**
Dorset Av. Glen —4A **18**
Dorset Av. Wig —6A **36**
Dorset St. Leic —5C **20**
Double Rail Clo. Wig —2G **45**
Doudney Clo. Sto S —4B **50**
Dovecote Clo. Sap —6B **50**
Dovecote Rd. Cft —6G **41**
Dovedale Av. Blab —4B **44**
Dovedale Ct. Leic —6G **29**
Dovedale Rd. Leic —6G **29**
Dovedale Rd. Thurm —4C **14**
Dover Ho. Leic —2C **28** (5E **5**)
Dove Rise. Oad —3C **38**
Dover St. Kib —5H **59**
Dover St. Leic —2C **28** (5E **5**)
Downham Av. Leic —3A **20**
Downing Dri. Leic —4C **30**
Down St. Leic —4D **20**
Draper St. Leic —4E **29**
Drayton Rd. Leic —6C **18**
Dribdale. Flec —6C **58**
Drinkstone Rd. Leic —2G **29**
Drive, The. Bir —5G **13**
Drive, The. Kib —5B **62**
Drive, The. Scrap —5F **23**
Driveway, The. Leic —2G **31**
Dronfield St. Leic —2E **29**
Drovers Way. Nar —4D **42**

Drove, The. Count —2C **54**
Drumcliffe Rd. Leic —1E **31**
Drummond Rd. End —6G **33**
Drummond Rd. Leic —2B **20**
Drury La. Oad —3H **37**
Dryden St. Leic —1C **28** (2E **4**)
Dudleston Clo. Leic —2A **30**
Dudley Av. Leic —1C **30**
Dudley Clo. Leic —1C **30**
Duffield Av. Wig —5D **36**
Duffield St. Leic —2E **29**
Dukes Clo. Thurm —4D **14**
Dukes Clo. Wig —6D **36**
Dukes Dri. Leic —5E **29**
Dukes Dri. Flats. Leic —5E **29**
Duke St. Leic —3B **28** (6D **5**)
Dulverton Clo. Wig —3B **46**
Dulverton Rd. Leic —2G **27**
Dumbleton Av. Leic —6G **27**
Dunbar Rd. Leic —3G **21**
Dunblane Av. Leic —1F **21**
Duncan Av. Hunc —3H **41**
Duncan Rd. Leic —2H **35**
Dundee Rd. Blab —5B **44**
Dundonald Rd. Leic —4C **20**
Dunholme Rd. Leic —4G **21**
Dunire Clo. Leic —2G **19**
Dunkirk St. Leic —3C **28** (6E **5**)
Dunlin Rd. Leic —6E **21**
Dunmore Rd. Blab —5B **44**
Duns La. Leic —2A **28** (5A **5**)
Dunstall Av. Leic —5B **26**
Dunster St. Leic —2F **27**
Dunsville Wlk. Leic —2F **21**
Dunton La. Dun B —6E **61**
Dunton Rd. B Ast —3D **60**
Dunton Rd. Leir —6B **60**
Dunton St. Leic —6H **19**
Dunton St. Wig —2F **45**
Dupont Clo. Glen —6B **18**
Dupont Gdns. Glen —6B **18**
Durham Dri. Wig —5C **36**
Durnford Rd. Wig —3A **46**
Durston Clo. Leic —3D **30**
Duxbury Rd. Leic —6G **21**
Dysart Way. Leic —5C **20**

Eagle Clo. B Ast —6A **52**
Ealing Rd. Leic —6B **28**
Eamont Clo. Leic —6H **35**
Eamont Grn. Leic —6H **35**
Earl Howe St. Leic —3D **28**
Earlhowe Ter. Leic —2H **27**
Earl Russell St. Leic —3G **35**
Earls Clo. Thurm —4D **14**
Earl Shilton Rd. Thurl —2A **40**
Earl Smith Clo. Whet —4A **44**
Earl St. Leic —1C **28** (2E **4**)
Earl's Way. Thurm —4D **14**
Earlswood Rd. Leic —4D **30**
East Av. Leic —5E **29**
East Av. Sys —6G **7**
East Av. Whet —3H **43**
E. Bond St. Leic
　　　　　—1B **28** (2C **4**)
Eastcourt Rd. Leic —3E **37**

Eastern Boulevd. Leic
　　　　　—4A **28** (7A **5**)
Eastfield Rd. Leic —2F **27**
Eastfield Rd. Thurm —3D **14**
East Gates. Leic —1B **28** (3C **4**)
E. Goscote Ind. Est. E Gos
　　　　　—2H **7**
Eastleigh Rd. Leic —4G **27**
East Link. Leic —2C **34**
Eastmere Rd. Wig —6H **37**
East Pk. Rd. Leic —3E **29**
East Rd. Bir —6G **13**
East St. Leic —2C **28** (5E **5**)
East St. Oad —3A **38**
East Wlk. Rat —4C **16**
Eastway Rd. Wig —5F **37**
Eastwood Rd. Leic —4H **35**
Ebchester Clo. Leic —6G **35**
Ebchester Rd. Leic —6G **35**
Edale Clo. Leic —4C **26**
Eddystone Rd. Leic —6E **23**
Eden Clo. Oad —3C **38**
Eden Gdns. Leic —4C **12**
Edenhall Clo. Leic —2F **21**
Edenhall Clo. Oad —5D **38**
Edenhurst Av. Leic —2D **34**
Eden Rd. Oad —3C **38**
Edensor St. Leic —2E **21**
Eden Way. Leic —1D **44**
Edgbaston Clo. Leic —4C **12**
Edgecote Ct. Leic —5G **21**
Edgehill Clo. Gt G —3D **48**
Edgehill Rd. Leic —3G **21**
Edgeley Rd. Count —1F **55**
Edith Av. Leic —2E **35**
Edmonton Rd. Leic
　　　　　—6C **20** (1F **4**)
Edward Av. Leic —1D **34**
Edward Clo. Oad —4C **38**
Edward Dri. Glen P —2E **45**
Edward Rd. Flec —6B **58**
Edward Rd. Leic —5D **28**
Edward St. Ans —5G **11**
Edward St. Leic —6E **21**
Egerton Av. Leic —3A **20**
Egginton St. Leic —3E **29**
Eider Clo. Whet —1H **53**
Eileen Av. Leic —3A **20**
Elbow La. Leic —1A **28** (2B **4**)
Eldon St. Leic —1C **28** (2E **4**)
Elfed Thomas Building. Leic
　　　　　—5C **5**
Elfin Gro. Dun B —5G **61**
Elgin Av. Leic —5D **18**
Elisha Clo. Sto S —3C **50**
Elizabeth Clo. Flec —6B **58**
Elizabeth Ct. Glen —4H **17**
Elizabeth Ct. Wig —1B **46**
Elizabeth Cres. Wig —5D **36**
Elizabeth Dri. Oad —5C **38**
Elizabeth Dri. Thurm —3C **14**
Elizabeth Gdns. Whet —4H **43**
Elizabeth Ho. Leic —6E **19**
Elizabeth Rd. Flec —6B **58**
Elizabeth St. Leic —2G **29**
Elland Rd. Lelc —2H **25**
Ellesmere Pl. Leic —5F **27**
Ellesmere Rd. Leic —5F **27**
Elliot Clo. Oad —5E **39**

Elliot Clo. Whet —1A **54**
Elliott Dri. Leic F —3H **25**
Elliott Dri. Thurm —5E **15**
Elliott Rd. Leic —1H **19**
Ellis Av. Leic —4C **20**
Ellis Clo. Glen —5H **17**
Ellis Dri. Leic F —4F **25**
Ellis Fields. Oad —5E **39**
Ellison Clo. Sto S —2B **50**
Ellison Clo. Wig —3F **45**
Ellis St. Ans —5F **11**
Ellwood Clo. Leic —3B **30**
Elm Clo. Grob —3F **17**
Elmcroft Av. Leic —6B **22**
Elmdale St. Leic —3C **20**
Elmfield Av. Bir —4F **13**
Elmfield Av. Leic —4E **29**
Elmfield Gdns. Leic —4E **29**
Elmhurst Clo. Nar —4C **42**
Elms Clo. Oad —4B **38**
Elms Ct. Leic —1E **37**
Elms La. Bur O —2H **49**
Elmsleigh Av. Leic —6F **29**
Elms Rd. Leic —6E **29**
Elms Rd. Houses. Leic —1F **37**
Elms, The. Blab —4B **44**
Elms, The. Count —1E **55**
Elmsthorpe Rise. Leic —4E **27**
Elm Tree Av. Glen —5G **17**
Elmtree Clo. Ham —3C **22**
Elm Tree Rd. Cosb —3E **53**
Elmwood Row. Leic —5C **36**
Elsadene Av. Leic —2C **20**
Elsadene Ct. Leic —6F **29**
Elsalene Dri. Grob —6G **9**
Elsham Clo. Leic —2B **26**
Elston Fields. Leic —3B **36**
Elstree Av. Leic —5E **23**
Elsworthy Wlk. Leic —1B **26**
Elwells Av. Dun B —5F **61**
Elwin Av. Wig —5F **37**
Emberton Clo. Wig —6H **37**
Emburn Ho. Leic —5D **18**
Emerson Clo. Leic —2E **19**
Emperor Way. Whet —1H **53**
Empire Rd. Leic —6H **19**
Enderby Rd. Thurl —6A **32**
Enderby Rd. Whet —2G **43**
Enderby Rd. Ind. Est. Whet
　　　　　—2H **43**
Englefield Rd. Leic —2D **30**
Ennerdale Clo. Oad —4E **39**
Ensbury Gdns. Leic —4B **30**
Eppington St. Leic —2D **28**
Epping Way. Leic —6G **35**
Epsom Rd. Leic —3D **20**
Equity Rd. End —6G **33**
Equity Rd. Leic —3H **27**
Erdyngton Rd. Leic —3D **26**
Eric Wood Building. Leic
　　　　　—3A **28** (6B **5**)
Erith Rd. Leic —6H **27**
Ernee Clo. Glen —6B **18**
Erskine St. Leic —1C **28** (2E **4**)
Ervington Ct. Leic —3B **34**
Ervin's Lock. Wig —3G **45**
Eskdale Clo. Oad —5D **38**
Eskdale Ho. Leic —6G **35**
Eskdale Rd. Leic —2H **19**

Essex Rd. Leic —4G **21**
Essex Rd. Wig —6B **36**
Estley Rd. B Ast —6A **52**
Estoril Av. Wig —5G **37**
Ethel Rd. Leic —3G **29**
Eton Clo. Leic —1D **36**
Eunice Av. Hunc —4H **41**
Euston St. Leic —6B **28**
Evelyn Dri. Leic —5G **27**
Evelyn Rd. Leic —5C **26**
Everard Way. Nar —4D **34**
Everest Ct. Leic —6D **20**
Everett Clo. Thurn —5E **15**
Everson Clo. B Ast —2B **60**
Every St. Leic —2B **28** (4D **4**)
Evesham Rd. Leic —5G **27**
Evington Clo. Leic —3G **29**
Evington Dri. Leic —4F **29**
Evington Footway. Leic
—3D **28**
Evington La. Leic —4F **29**
Evington Parks Rd. Leic
—4F **29**
Evington Pl. Leic —3E **29**
Evington Rd. Leic —3D **28**
Evington Valley Rd. Leic
—4F **29**
Exchange, The. Leic —5A **36**
Exeter Rd. Wig —5D **36**
Exmoor Av. Leic —5H **19**
Exmoor Clo. Wig —2B **46**
Exton Rd. Leic —6G **21**
Eynsford Clo. Leic —1G **37**

Fairbourne Rd. Leic —6E **27**
Fairburn Ho. Leic —5D **18**
Faircharm Trading Est. Leic
—5H **27**
Fairefield Cres. Glen —3B **18**
Faire Rd. Glen —4B **18**
Fairestone Av. Glen —5A **18**
Fairfax Clo. Leic —3G **21**
Fairfax Ct. Gt G —3D **48**
Fairfax Rd. Leic —3G **21**
Fairfield Rd. Oad —3B **38**
Fairfield St. Leic —2E **29**
Fairfield St. Wig —1F **45**
Fairford Av. Leic —4B **30**
Fairhaven Rd. Ans —4G **11**
Fairholme Rd. Leic —3D **36**
Fairisle Way. Count —2F **55**
Fairstone Hill. Oad —5B **38**
Fairview Av. Whet —4H **43**
Fairway. Kib —5B **62**
Fairway, The. Blab —4A **44**
Fairway, The. Kir M —3F **25**
Fairway, The. Leic —3B **36**
Fairway, The. Oad —6H **29**
Falcon Clo. B Ast —6A **52**
Falcon Clo. Leic F —5E **25**
Falconer Cres. Leic —5C **18**
Falcon Rd. Ans —6E **11**
Faldo Clo. Leic —6C **14**
Fallow Clo. Whet —6H **43**
Fallowfield Rd. Leic —3D **30**
Falmouth Dri. Wig —2A **46**
Falmouth Rd. Leic —3H **29**
Faraday Clo. B Ast —3B **60**

Farleigh Av. Wig —5F **37**
Farleigh Clo. B Ast —6A **52**
Farley Rd. Leic —1F **37**
Farley Way. Kir M —1F **25**
Farm Clo. Bir —4H **13**
Farm Clo. L'thrpe —5E **43**
Farm Clo., The. Leic —4B **36**
Farmers Clo. Glen —5G **17**
Farmway. Leic —3C **34**
Farndale. Wig —1D **46**
Farndon Rd. Sto S —3B **50**
Farnham St. Leic   1E **29**
Farnworth Clo. Leic —2F **21**
Farrier La. Leic —2F **19**
Farrier's Way. E Gos —2H **7**
Farringdon St. Leic —6E **21**
Farr Wood Clo. Grob —2E **17**
Farthingdale Clo. Cosb —2G **53**
Fastnet Rd. Leic —6E **23**
(in two parts)
Faversham Clo. Leic —1A **26**
Fayrhurst Rd. Leic —3A **36**
Featherby Dri. Glen P —6E **35**
Featherstone Dri. Leic —1C **44**
Feature Rd. Thurn —2C **14**
Federation St. End —6G **33**
Felley Way. Leic —5G **19**
Felstead Rd. Leic —1H **19**
Fenners Clo. Leic —4C **12**
Fenton Clo. Oad —6A **38**
Fenwick Rd. Oad —5E **39**
Fermain Clo. Leic —2D **30**
Fern Bank. Leic —1E **29**
Fern Clo. Thurn —2E **31**
Fern Cres. Grob —1D **16**
Ferndale Dri. Rat —5D **16**
Ferndale Rd. Leic —3D **36**
Ferndale Rd. Thurm —5C **14**
Ferndown Clo. Leic —1A **26**
Ferne Clo. Oad —5C **38**
Fernhurst Rd. Leic —1D **34**
Fernie Dene. Gt G —2E **49**
Fernie Rd. Leic —6F **21**
Fernlea. Nar —2B **42**
Fernleys Clo. Leic —2F **19**
Fern Rise. Leic —4C **22**
Ferrars Ct. Braun —6B **26**
Ferrers Rise. Grob —2E **17**
Ferrers St. Leic —4B **36**
Ferrous Clo. Leic —5E **21**
Festival Av. Thurn —5B **14**
Field Clo. L'thrpe —4E **43**
Field Ct. Rd. Grob —2F **17**
Fieldfare Wlk. Leic —6E **21**
Fieldgate Cres. Bir —3E **13**
Fieldhouse Rd. Leic —2D **20**
Fieldhurst Av. Leic —1C **34**
Fielding Rd. Bir —4F **13**
Field View. Sys —6C **6**
Field View. Thurm —4E **15**
Fieldway Cres. Gt G —2D **48**
Fieldway, The. B Ast —2B **60**
Filbert St. Leic —4A **28**
Filbert St. E. Leic
—4B **28** (8C **5**)
Finch Clo. Leic —2C **26**
Finch Way. Nar —4C **42**
Fineshade Av. Leic —5G **19**
Finsbury Rd. Leic —4E **21**

Finson Clo. Wig —6F **37**
Fiona Dri. Thurn —2F **31**
Firfield Av. Bir —4G **13**
Fir Tree Av. Count —1E **55**
Fir Tree Clo. Wig —4E **37**
Firtree La. Grob —1E **17**
Firtree Wlk. Grob —2E **17**
Fisher Clo. Costn —1B **6**
Fisher Clo. Sto S —3A **50**
Fishley Clo. Glen —6H **17**
Fishponds Clo. Glen —5H **17**
Fishpools. Leic —2C **34**
Fitzroy St. Leic —2H **27**
Fitzwilliam Clo. Oad —5D **38**
Flamborough Rd. Leic —6D **22**
Flamingo Dri. Whet —1H **53**
Flatholme Rd. Leic —5E **23**
Flax Rd. Leic —3D **20**
Flaxfield Clo. Grob —2F **17**
Flax Rd. Leic —3D **20**
Fleckney Ind. Est. Flec —6C **58**
Fleckney Rd. Kib —5F **59**
Fleckney Rd. Kilb —3E **57**
Fleet St. Leic —1C **28** (2E **4**)
Fleet, The. Sto S —1C **50**
Fleetwood Rd. Leic —6C **28**
Fletcher Building. Leic —6A **5**
Fletcher Mall. Leic —1E **19**
Fletcher Rd. Sto S   2C **50**
Fletchers Clo. Nar —4D **42**
Fletchers Way. E Gos —2H **7**
Fletcher Way. E Gos —2H **7**
Flora St. Leic —2H **27**
Florence Av. Wig —2G **45**
Florence Rd. Leic —1E **29**
Florence St. Leic —2A **36**
Florence Wragg Way. Oad
—5D **38**
Floyd Clo. Leic —6C **14**
Fludes La. Oad —4C **38**
Folville Rise. Leic —5E **27**
Fontwell Dri. Leic —5F **35**
Forbes Clo. Glen —6A **18**
Ford Clo. Leic —6G **35**
Ford Rise. Leic —6G **35**
Ford, The. Glen P —3C **44**
Fordview Clo. Gt G —2C **48**
Forest Av. Thurn —3B **14**
Forest Clo. Grob —2D **16**
Forest Dri. Kir M —3E **25**
Foresters Clo. Glen —5H **17**
Foresters Row. E Gos —2H **7**
Forest Farm. Leic F —6E **25**
Forest Ho. La. Leic F —6E **25**
Forest Rise. Grob —2D **16**
Forest Rise. Leic F —4F **25**
Forest Rise. Oad —3C **38**
Forest Rise. Thurn —2F **31**
Forest Rd. End —4F **33**
Forest Rd. Hunc —3H **41**
Forest Rd. Leic —5E **21**
Forest Rd. Mark —2A **8**
Forest View. Grob —2D **16**
Forestway. Leic —5F **19**
Forge Clo. Glen —5G **17**
Forge Corner. Blab —3B **44**
Forrester Clo. Cosb —2G **53**
Forryan Clo. Cosb —3F **53**

Forryans Clo. Wig —2C **46**
Fosse Clo. End —1F **43**
Fosse La. Leic —6G **19**
Fosse Pk. Av. Leic —4D **34**
Fosse Pk. Shopping Cen. Leic
—4D **34**
Fosse Rd. Central. Leic —2G **27**
Fosse Rd. N. Leic —1G **27**
Fosse Rd. S. Leic —5F **27**
Fosse Way. Sys —1D **14**
Foston Ga. Wig —3C **46**
Foston La. Count —6H **55**
Foston Rd. Count —1F **55**
Foundry La. Leic —6C **20**
Foundry La. Sys —6D **6**
Foundry Sq. Leic —6C **20**
Fountains Av. Leic —6H **35**
Fowler Clo. Leic —1G **19**
Fox Covert. Whet —6H **43**
Foxcroft Clo. Leic —1G **35**
Fox End. Thurl —6A **32**
Foxglove Clo. E Gos —2H **7**
Foxglove Clo. Nar —3C **42**
Foxglove Rd. Ham —3C **22**
Foxhill Dri. Glen P —6E **35**
Foxholes Rd. Leic —3B **26**
Fox Hollow. E Gos —1H **7**
Foxhunter Dri. Oad —3H **37**
Fox La. Kir M —2D **24**
Fox La. Leic —1B **28** (3D **4**)
Foxon St. Leic —2H **27**
Foxon Way. Leic —6B **26**
Fox St. Leic —2C **28** (4F **4**)
Foxton Lock Clo. Wig —3G **45**
Framland Ho. Leic —2D **28**
Frampton Av. Leic —2F **27**
Franche Rd. Leic —1G **27**
Francis Av. Leic —2D **34**
Francis Ct. Leic —3G **35**
Francis St. Leic —6F **29**
Francis Wlk. Leic —5G **29**
Frankel Cres. Wig —2C **46**
Franklin Way. Whet —1H **53**
Franklyn Rd. Leic —3F **35**
Frankson Av. Leic —6E **27**
Fraser Clo. Leic —6C **20** (1F **4**)
Frederick Rd. Leic —1E **29**
Fredrick St. Wig —6F **37**
Fredscott Clo. Leic —6E **23**
Freeboard Rd. Leic —2D **34**
Freehold Rd. Bir —6G **13**
Freehold St. Leic —6D **29**
Free La. Leic —1B **28** (3D **4**)
Freeman Rd. N. Leic —6H **21**
Freemans Ct. Rat —5D **16**
Freeman's Way. E Gos —1H **7**
Freemantle Rd. Leic —6G **29**
Freemen's Comn. Rd. Leic
—5B **28**
Freemen's Comn. Trading Est.
Leic —5B **28**
Freemen's Holt. Leic —2G **35**
Freer Clo. Blab —3B **44**
Freer Clo. Wig —3C **46**
Freeschool La. Leic
—1A **28** (3B **4**)
French Rd. Leic —6G **21**
Frenshaw Clo. Oad —5A **38**
Freshwater Clo. Wig —4B **46**

Frevin St. Leic —6G **21**
Frewen Dri. Sap —5B **50**
Friar La. Leic —2A **28** (5B **5**)
Friars Causeway. Leic
—1A **28** (3A **4**)
Friday St. Leic —6A **20** (1B **4**)
(in two parts)
Frinton Av. Leic —3D **30**
Frisby Rd. Leic —5E **21**
Fritchley Clo. Hunc —4A **42**
Frith Clo. Glen —5A **18**
Froanes Clo. End —5G **33**
Frog Island. Leic
—6A **20** (1A **4**)
Frolesworth Rd. B Ast —3A **60**
Frolesworth Rd. Leic —6C **18**
Frolesworth Rd. Leir —6A **60**
Frolesworth Way. Leic —1C **26**
Frome Av. Oad —3D **38**
Front St. Bir —5H **13**
Fulbeck Av. Leic —3D **30**
Fulford Rd. Leic —2A **26**
Fullhurst Av. Leic —4F **27**
Fulmar Rd. Ans —6F **11**
Furlongs Clo. Sys —6G **7**
Furrows Clo. L'thrpe —5F **43**

Gables Hall, The. Oad —1H **37**
Gaddesby Av. Leic —4G **27**
Gainsborough Rd. Kib —4A **62**
Gainsborough Rd. Leic —1C **36**
Gainsborough Wlk. Leic
—1A **30**
Galahad Clo. Leic F —5G **25**
Galaxy Wlk. Leic —2E **29**
Galby St. Leic —6F **21**
Gallards Hill. Leic —4B **26**
(in three parts)
Galleywood Dri. Leic —3H **19**
Gallimore Clo. Glen —4C **18**
Gallowtree Ga. Leic
—1B **28** (3D **4**)
Galsworthy Ct. Leic —2E **27**
Galway Rd. Leic —6E **13**
Gamel Rd. Leic —2B **30**
Gamel Wlk. Leic —2B **30**
Ganton Rd. Leic —1A **26**
Garden Clo. Oad —4A **38**
Gardenfield Rd. Leic —1H **21**
Garden St. Leic —6B **20** (1D **4**)
Garden St. Thurm —4C **14**
Garden St. Wig —2F **45**
Garendon St. Leic —1D **28**
Garendon Way. Grob —3E **17**
Garfield Pk. Gt G —1D **48**
Garfield St. Leic —5C **20**
Garfit Rd. Kir M —2E **25**
Garland Cres. Leic —5F **19**
Garnett Cres. Leic —6G **35**
Garsdale. Wig —1D **46**
Garth Av. Leic —1A **20**
Gartree Rd. Leic —6H **29**
(in two parts)
Gaskell Wlk. Leic —2E **27**
Gas La. Wig —2A **46**
Gas St. Leic —6B **20**
Gateway Building. Leic
—3A **28** (6B **5**)

Gateway St. Leic —3A **28** (6B **5**)
Gateway, The. Leic
—3A **28** (6B **5**)
Gaulby La. Stoug —1D **38**
Gaul St. Leic —3H **27**
Gayhurst Clo. Leic —2D **34**
Gayhurst Clo. Wig —1C **46**
Gayton Av. Leic —4E **21**
Gayton Heights. End —6G **33**
G.E.C. Ind. Est. Whet —5G **43**
Gedding Rd. Leic —2G **29**
Geddington Clo. Wig —1C **46**
Gedge Way. Leic —3A **36**
Gees Lock Clo. Leic —5F **35**
Gelert Av. Leic —1D **30**
Georgeham Clo. Wig —2B **46**
George Hill Clo. Sto S —2B **50**
George Marriott Clo. Sto S
—4A **50**
George St. Ans —5F **11**
George St. End —6G **33**
George St. Leic —6C **20** (1E **4**)
George Toon Ct. Sys —5E **7**
Gervas Rd. Leic —6C **22**
Gibbon's Clo. Leic —5C **20**
Gibson Clo. Wig —6F **37**
Gifford Clo. Leic —4B **30**
Gilbert Clo. Leic —1G **21**
Gilbert Murray Hall. Oad
—1H **37**
Gillam Butts. Count —2E **55**
Gillbank Dri. Rat —5C **16**
Gilliver St. Leic —1D **36**
Gillman Rd. Leic —5E **19**
Gilmorton Av. Leic —5F **35**
Gilmorton Clo. Leic —5F **35**
Gilmour Clo. Leic —6B **12**
Gilstead Clo. Thurn —3F **31**
Gimson Av. Cosb —2F **53**
Gimson Clo. Leic —4A **22**
Gimson Rd. Leic —1F **27**
Gipsy La. Leic & Hum —3E **21**
Gipsy Rd. Leic —3D **20**
Gisbourne Ct. Evi —5A **30**
Glade, The. Leic —2D **34**
Gladstone St. Ans —5G **11**
Gladstone St. Flec —6B **58**
Gladstone St. Kib —5G **59**
Gladstone St. Leic
—1C **28** (2E **4**)
Gladstone St. Wig —6F **37**
Glaisdale Clo. Leic —2G **19**
Glaisdale Rd. Wig —2D **46**
Glamorgan Av. Wig —1F **45**
Glazebrook Rd. Leic —4D **18**
Glazebrook Sq. Leic —5E **19**
Glebe Clo. Glen —5H **17**
Glebe Clo. Leic —1G **37**
Glebe Clo. Wig —6F **37**
Glebe Cotts. Oad —1G **37**
Glebe Dri. Count —2D **54**
Glebelands Rd. Leic —3D **12**
Glebelands, The. Gt G —3C **48**
Glebe Rd. B Ast —1A **60**
Glebe Rd. Grob —2E **17**
Glebe Rd. Leic —2G **37**
Glebe St. Leic —2C **28** (5F **5**)
Glebe Way. Sys —5C **6**
Glenbarr Av. Leic —5H **19**

Glenborne Rd. Leic —5C **36**
Glencoe Av. Leic —1E **21**
Glendale Av. Glen —2H **17**
Glendon St. Leic —4D **20**
Glendower Clo. Leic —1B **30**
Gleneagles Av. Leic —2F **21**
Gleneagles Wlk. Leic —1E **21**
Glenfield Cres. Glen —5A **18**
Glenfield Frith Dri. Glen —4B **18**
Glenfield La. Kir M —1E **25**
Glenfield Rd. Leic —6C **18**
Glenfield Rd. E. Leic —2G **27**
Glenfrith Clo. Leic —2D **18**
Glenfrith Way. Leic —4D **18**
Glengarry Clo. Leic —6E **19**
Glengarry Ct. Leic —6D **18**
Glengarry Way. Leic —5D **18**
Glengate. Wig —1F **45**
Glenhills Boulevd. Leic —4G **35**
(in three parts)
Glenhills Way. Leic —4G **35**
Glenmore Rd. Leic —2F **21**
Glen Pk. Av. Glen —3H **17**
Glen Rise. Glen P —5F **35**
Glen Rise. Oad —1A **48**
Glen Rd. New H —4A **48**
Glen Rd. Oad —4C **38**
Glenrothes Clo. Leic —2A **26**
Glen St. Leic —3D **20**
Glenville Av. Glen —3A **18**
Glenville Av. Glen P —1B **44**
Glen Way. Oad —5C **38**
Glenwood Clo. Leic —6F **29**
Glossop St. Leic —3E **29**
Gloucester Av. Sys —5G **7**
Gloucester Cres. Wig —6A **36**
Glover Ct. Leic —3G **35**
Glovers Wlk. Leic —1G **19**
Goddards Clo. Kilb —2E **57**
Goddards Clo. Leic —3F **19**
Goddards Clo. Oad —4H **37**
Godfrey Clo. Leic —5B **12**
Godstow Wlk. Leic —1A **30**
Godwin Av. Wig —1C **46**
Goldhill. Leic —4C **36**
Goldhill Rd. Leic —2F **37**
Golf Course La. Leic —2A **26**
Goode's Av. Sys —1E **15**
Goode's La. Sys —6E **7**
Gooding Av. Leic —3D **26**
(in four parts)
Gooding Clo. Leic —4F **27**
Goodwin Ho. Leic —6D **20**
Goodwood Cres. Leic —2B **30**
Goodwood Rd. Leic —1B **30**
Gopsall St. Leic —3D **28**
Gordon Av. Leic —3D **28**
Gordon Ho. Leic —2D **28**
Gorham Rise. B Ast —6H **51**
Gorseburn Ho. Leic —5D **18**
Gorse Hill. Ans —6G **11**
(in two parts)
Gorse Hill Ind. Est. Leic
—1E **19**
Gorse La. Oad —6D **38**
Gorse La. Sys —6D **6**
Gorsty Clo. Leic —2F **19**
Goscote Hall Rd. Bir —5F **13**
Goshawk Clo. B Ast —6A **52**

Gosling St. Leic —3A **28** (6B **5**)
Gotham St. Leic —3D **28**
Gough Rd. Leic —1G **29**
Gower St. Leic —6B **20** (1D **4**)
Goy Gdns. Leic —1C **28** (2F **4**)
Grace Gdns. Leic —2A **36**
Grace Rd. Leic —1A **36**
Grace Rd. Sap —5C **50**
Grafton Dri. Wig —1D **46**
Grafton Pl. Leic —6B **20** (1C **4**)
Graham St. Leic —1D **28**
Grampian Clo. Leic —2B **36**
Granary Clo. Glen —6H **17**
Granary Clo. Kib —6A **62**
Granby Av. Leic —1F **29**
Granby Bldgs. Leic —4D **4**
Granby Pl. Leic —2B **28** (4D **4**)
Granby Rd. Leic —2H **35**
Granby St. Leic —2B **28** (4D **4**)
Grange Av. Leic F —4H **25**
Grange Bus. Pk., The. Whet
—2H **43**
Grange Clo. Glen —5H **17**
Grange Clo. Gt G —2D **48**
Grange Clo. Rat —5D **16**
Grange Dri. Glen P —6F **35**
Grange Dri. Whet —3H **43**
Grange La. Leic —3A **28** (6B **5**)
Grange La. Thurn —3E **31**
Grange Pk. Thurn —3E **31**
Grange Rd. B Ast —1A **60**
Grange Rd. Wig —4E **37**
Grange, The. Nar —4E **43**
Grangeway Rd. Wig —5E **37**
Grantham Av. B Ast —5H **51**
Grantham Rd. Leic —5C **22**
Grant Way. Leic —5A **36**
Granville Av. Oad —3H **37**
Granville Cres. Wig —4D **36**
Granville Rd. Leic —4D **28**
Granville Rd. Wig —4D **36**
Grape St. Leic —1A **28** (2B **4**)
Grasmere Rd. Wig —6H **37**
Grasmere St. Leic
—3A **28** (7A **5**)
Grass Acres. Leic —2C **34**
Grassington Clo. Leic —2G **19**
Grassington Dri. Wig —1D **46**
Grassy La. Mark —3A **8**
Gravel St. Leic —1B **28** (2C **4**)
Gravel, The. Bur O —3H **49**
Graylyn Ct. Thurm —5C **14**
Grays Ct. Nar —6G **33**
Gray St. Leic —3A **28** (6A **5**)
Grayswood Dri. Leic —4A **12**
Gt. Arler Rd. Leic —1C **36**
Gt. Central St. Leic
—1A **28** (2A **4**)
Gt. Central Way. Leic —1H **43**
Gt. Meadow Rd. Leic —3F **19**
Grebe Way. Whet —6H **43**
Greenacre Dri. Leic —2B **30**
Greenbank Dri. Oad —4B **38**
Greenbank Rd. Leic —4D **22**
Greencoat Rd. Leic —6C **18**
Greencroft. Sto S —4B **50**
Greendale Rd. Glen P —6F **35**
Greenfields. Whet —4H **43**
Greengate La. Bir —4D **12**

Greenhill Clo. Nar —4C **42**
Greenhill Rd. Leic —6C **28**
Greenhithe Rd. Leic —6H **27**
Greenhithe Wlk. Leic —6A **28**
Greenland Av. Leic —5A **22**
Greenland Dri. Leic —5A **22**
Green La. Count —1F **55**
Green La. Clo. Leic —1H **29**
Green La. Rd. Leic —6F **21**
Green Rd. B Ast —6A **52**
(in two parts)
Greenside Pl. Leic —4B **36**
Green, Tho. Blab —3C **44**
Green, The. Cft —6G **41**
Green, The. Hunc —4H **41**
Green, The. Mark —2B **8**
Green, The. Sys —5F **7**
Green Wlk. Leic —2C **26**
Greenway. Kib —5B **62**
Greenway, The. Leic —4C **20**
Greenwich Clo. Nar —3D **42**
Greenwood Rd. Leic —1H **29**
Gregory Clo. Thurm —4E **15**
Gregory's Clo. Braun —6R **26**
Gregson Clo. Leic —6B **14**
Grendon Clo. Wig —6G **37**
Grenfell Rd. Leic —1G **37**
Grenfell Wlk. Leic —1G **37**
Gresley Clo. Leic —1G **19**
Gresley Clo. Thurn —1F **31**
Gretna Way. Leic —6E **23**
Grey Clo. Grob —2F **17**
Grey Cres. New L —2H **9**
Grey Friars. Leic
—2B **28** (4C **4**)
Greylag Clo. Whet —1H **53**
Greylands Paddock. Grob
—2F **17**
Greys Dri. Grob —3E **17**
Greystoke Clo. Leic —2A **20**
Greystoke Wlk. Leic —2A **20**
Greystone Av. Leic —1B **30**
Grisedale Clo. Leic —4A **28**
Grizedale Gro. Nar —2B **42**
Groby La. New L —4H **9**
Groby Rd. Ans —1A **18**
Groby Rd. Glen —2H **17**
(in two parts)
Groby Rd. Rat —4C **16**
Groby Rd. Glenfield. Glen
—2A **18**
Grocot Rd. Leic —4A **30**
Grosvenor Clo. Glen P —2D **44**
Grosvenor Cres. Leic —2H **37**
Grosvenor St. Leic
—6C **20** (1E **4**)
Grovebury Rd. Leic —2A **20**
Grovebury Wlk. Leic —2B **20**
Grove Farm Triangle. End
—4C **34**
Grove Rd. Leic —1E **29**
Grove Rd. Whet —5H **43**
Grove Way. Nar —5D **34**
Guildford St. Leic —3E **29**
Guildhall La. Leic
—2A **28** (4B **4**)
Guilford Dri. Wig —4D **36**
Guilford Rd. Leic —1F **37**
Gullet La. Kir M —3C **24**

Gumley Sq. End —6H **33**
Gunthorpe Rd. Leic —3B **26**
Gurnell Rd. Leic —1E **19**
Gurney Cres. L'thrpe —5E **43**
Guthlaxton Av. Leic —2D **28**
Guthlaxton St. Leic —2D **28**
Guthlaxton Way. Wig —3C **46**
Guthridge Cres. Leic —4F **27**
Gwencole Av. Leic —1E **35**
Gwencole Cres. Leic —2E **35**
Gwendolen Rd. Leic —2F **29**
(in two parts)
Gwendolen Rd. Gdns. Leic
—2G **29**
Gwendolin Av. Bir —4H **13**
Gwendoline Dri. Count —1D **54**
Gynsill La. Ans —2B **18**
(in two parts)

Hackett Rd. Leic —5D **18**
Haddenham Rd. Leic —5G **27**
Haddon Clo. Sys —6D **6**
Haddon St. Leic —2E **29**
Hadrian Clo. Sys —1C **14**
Hadrian Rd. Leic —6D **12**
Hadrian Rd. Thurm —4C **14**
Haig Pl. Leic —5E **27**
Halcroft Rise. Wig —2B **46**
Halcroft, The. Sys —5E **7**
Half Moon Cres. Oad —2C **38**
Halford Clo. Gt G —3D **48**
Halford Clo. Whet —5H **43**
Halford Rd. Kib —5H **59**
Halford St. Leic —2B **28** (4D **4**)
Haltord St. Sys —6E **7**
Halifax Dri. Leic —2A **20**
Halkin St. Leic —4D **20**
Hallam Av. Bir —4F **13**
Hallam Cres. E. Leic —5D **26**
Hallaton Rd. Leic —5H **21**
Hallaton St. Leic —2A **36**
Hallbrook Rd. B Ast —3B **60**
Hall Clo. Glen P —6F **35**
Hall Clo. Kib —4H **59**
Hallcroft Av. Count —2E **55**
Hallcroft Gdns. Count —2E **55**
Hall Dri. Oad —3B **38**
Halley Clo. Leic —5A **12**
Hall Farm Cres. B Ast —2C **60**
Hall Farm Rd. Thurc —1B **12**
Hall Gdns. Gt G —3D **48**
Hall La. Leic —2G **35**
Hall Rd. Scrap —5F **23**
Halls Ct. Leic —3C **30**
Hall Wlk. End —5H **33**
Halsbury St. Leic —4F **29**
Halstead St. Leic —1F **29**
Halter Slade. Wig —2C **46**
Hambledon Grn. Leic —6D **12**
Hamble Rd. Oad —3C **38**
Hambleton Clo. Leic F —5F **25**
Hamelin Rd. Leic —2D **26**
Hamilton Bungalow. Leic
—4E **23**
Hamilton Bus. Pk. Leic —1B **22**
(in two parts)
Hamilton La. Scrap —3E **23**

Hamilton St. Leic —3D **28**
Hammercliffe Rd. Leic —5E **21**
Hampden Rd. Leic —3G **21**
Hampshire Rd. Leic —2H **35**
Hampstead Clo. Leic —3D **42**
Hampton Clo. Glen P —2D **44**
Hampton Clo. Wig —1C **46**
Hanbury Rd. Leic —3D **30**
Handley St. Leic —2A **36**
Hannam Ct. Leic
—1B **28** (2D **4**)
Hanover Clo. Leic —4B **22**
Hansen Ct. Wig —1G **45**
Haramead Rd. Leic —6D **20**
Harborough Rd. Kib —4A **62**
Harborough Rd. Oad —3A **38**
Harcourt Clo. Sys —5E **7**
Harcourt Rd. Kib —5H **59**
Harcourt Rd. Wig —2C **46**
Harcourt Way. Leic —3B **34**
Hardie Cres. Leic —5B **26**
Harding St. Leic —6A **20** (1A **4**)
Harding Wlk. Leic
—6A **20** (1A **4**)
Hardwick Ct. Leic —4G **27**
Hardwick Cres. Sys —6D **6**
Hardwicke Rd. Nar —3B **42**
Hardwick Rd. Leic —3E **31**
Hardy's Av. Leic —1E **21**
Harebell Clo. Ham —2B **22**
Harecroft Cres. Sap —5C **50**
Harefield Av. Leic —1F **35**
Harene Cres. Leic Γ —4E **25**
Harewood St. Leic —6F **21**
Harland Clo. Cosb —2F **53**
Harlaxton St. Leic —5F **27**
Harlaxton Wlk. Leic —5G **27**
Harlequin Way. Whet —1H **53**
Harold's La. End —5H **33**
Harold St. Leic —1A **36**
Harrier Clo. B Ast —6A **52**
Harrington Rd. Wig —6G **37**
Harrington St. Leic —5E **21**
Harringworth Rd. Leic —3B **30**
Harris Clo. B Ast —2B **60**
Harris Grn. Leic —4A **26**
Harrison Clo. Glen —5A **18**
Harrison Clo. Whet —6A **44**
Harrison Clo. Wig —2H **45**
Harrison Rd. Leic —5D **20**
Harrisons Row. Sys —5F **7**
Harrison St. Thurm —3C **14**
Harris Rd. Leic —2F **19**
Harrogate Rd. Leic —4E **21**
Harrogate Way. Wig —2C **46**
Harrow Clo. Leic F —6F **25**
Harrowden Ct. Leic —1A **30**
Harrowden Rise. Leic —1A **30**
Harrowgate Dri. Bir —2E **13**
Harrow Rd. Leic —3G **27**
Hart Clo. Whet —6H **43**
Hartfield Rd. Leic —5D **22**
Hartington Rd. Leic —1E **29**
Hartopp Rd. Leic —5D **28**
Hart Rd. Leic —1E **29**
Hartshorn Clo. Thurm —5D **14**
Harvard Clo. Oad —3B **38**

Harvest Clo. Leic —2F **19**
Harvest Clo. L'thrpe —5F **43**
Harvester Clo. Leic F —5F **25**
Harvesters Corner. E Gos
—2H **7**
Harvest Way. B Ast —3B **60**
Harvey Wlk. Leic —2A **28** (4A **4**)
Harwin Rd. Leic —3B **30**
Hassal Rd. Leic —5C **18**
Hastings Rd. Kir M —3E **25**
Hastings Rd. Leic —5F **21**
Hastings, The. Braun —6B **26**
Hastings Wlk. Leic —6C **26**
Hathaway Av. Leic —6D **26**
Hatherleigh Rd. Leic —4H **29**
Hat Rd. Leic —2C **34**
Hattern Av. Leic —1H **19**
Havelock St. Leic
—3A **28** (7B **5**)
Haven Clo. Leic F —5F **25**
Havencrest Dri. Leic —6B **22**
Haven Wlk. Leic —1E **31**
Hawarden Av. Leic —6H **21**
Hawk Clo. B Ast —6A **52**
Hawker Rd. Oad —5E **39**
Hawkesbury Rd. Leic —2A **36**
Hawkes Hill. Leic —4B **36**
Hawthorn Av. Bir —3H **13**
Hawthorn Clo. Leic F —5E **25**
Hawthorn Dri. Blab —5B **44**
Hawthorne Dri. Leic —5A **30**
Hawthorne St. Leic —6F **19**
Hawthorn Rise. Grob —2F **17**
Hawthorns, The. Count —1E **55**
Hawthorns, The. Leic —6F **29**
Hawthorns, The. Mark —3C **8**
Haybarn Clo. L'thrpe —5F **43**
Hayden Av. Oad —5D **38**
Hayden Clo. Leic —2A **20**
Hayes Rd. Wig —6G **37**
Hayfield Clo. Glen —5H **17**
Hayling Cres. Leic —5A **22**
Haymarket. Leic
—1B **28** (3D **4**)
Haymarket Cen. Leic
—1B **28** (3D **4**)
Haynes Rd. Leic —6G **21**
Haywood Clo. Leic —3B **30**
Hazelbank Clo. Leic —3H **19**
Hazelbank Rd. Count —1F **55**
Hazel Clo. Bir —3H **13**
Hazel Clo. L'thrpe —5E **43**
Hazeldene Rd. Ham —3D **22**
Hazel Dri. Leic —3D **34**
Hazelhead Rd. Ans —5E **11**
Hazelnut Clo. Leic —3B **30**
Hazel St. Leic —4B **28**
Hazelwood Rd. Leic —4F **29**
Hazelwood Rd. Wig —3G **45**
Hazlemere Clo. Blab —4B **44**
Heacham Dri. Leic —2F **19**
Headingley Clo. Leic —4C **12**
Headland Rd. Leic —4A **30**
Headley Rd. Leic —2D **34**
Healey St. Wig —2F **45**
Healy Clo. Leic —1H **19**
Heanor St. Leic —6A **20** (1B **4**)
Heards Clo. Wig —3C **46**

Heard Wlk. Leic —1G **19**
Heath Av. Nar —1G **43**
Heath Av. Sys —6D **6**
Heathbrook Dri. Rat —5D **16**
Heathcott Rd. Leic —2A **36**
Heatherbrook Rd. Leic —6H **11**
Heather Rd. Leic —1C **36**
Heather Way. Count —2F **55**
Heathfield Rd. Wig —4F **37**
Heathgate Clo. Bir —3F **13**
Heathley Clo. Leic F —5F **25**
Heawood Way. Braun —6B **26**
Heays Clo. Leic —5C **18**
Hebden Clo. Leic —1C **44**
Heddington Clo. Leic —4C **36**
Heddington Way. Leic —4C **36**
Hedgerow La. Kir M —2D **24**
Hefford Gdns. Leic —1H **19**
Heighton Cres. L'thrpe —5E **43**
Helena Cres. Leic —1A **20**
Helmsley Rd. Leic —4B **36**
Helston Clo. Wig —2A **46**
Hemington Rd. Leic —4D **30**
Hemlock Clo. Nar —2B **42**
Henley Cres. Leic —6D **26**
Henley Rd. Leic —1G **27**
Henray Av. Leic —1C **44**
Henry Clo. Leic F —5F **25**
Henshaw St. Leic
—3B **28** (6C **5**)
Henson Clo. Bir —5F **13**
Henton Rd. Leic —2G **27**
Herbert Av. Leic —3D **20**
Herbert Clo. Whet —4A **44**
Herdsmans Clo. L'thrpe —4F **43**
Hereford Rd. Leic —2H **35**
Hereward Dri. Thurn —2F **31**
Herle Av. Leic —5D **26**
Herle Wlk. Leic —5D **26**
Hermitage Clo. Oad —4A **38**
Hermitage Rd. Bir —6G **13**
Heron Clo. Gt G —2C **48**
Heron Rd. Leic —6E **21**
Heron's Way. E Gos —1H **7**
Heron Way. Nar —1F **43**
Heron Way. Sys —5D **6**
Herrick Clo. End —6G **33**
Herrick Dri. Thurn —2F **31**
Herrick Rd. Leic —1C **36**
Herricks Av. Leic —6D **14**
Herrick Way. Wig —2C **46**
Herschell St. Leic —4E **29**
Herthull Rd. Leic —1C **30**
Hesilrige Wlk. Leic —5B **22**
Hesketh Av. Leic —6G **35**
Hesketh Clo. Leic —6G **35**
Hewes Clo. Glen P —6E **35**
Hewett Clo. Gt G —3C **48**
Hewitt Dri. Kir M —3F **25**
Hextall Rd. Leic —4A **30**
Heybrook Av. Blab —4A **44**
Heyford Rd. Leic —3B **26**
Heythrop Clo. Oad —5D **38**
Heyworth Rd. Leic —6G **27**
Hidcote Rd. Oad —5A **38**
Higgs Clo. Leic —2A **30**
Highbrow. Gt G —3E **49**
Highbury Rd. Leic —5E **21**
Highcliffe Rd. Ham —2A **22**

Highcroft Av. Oad —4C **38**
Highcroft Rd. Oad —6D **38**
Highcross St. Leic
(in two parts) —1A **28** (2A **4**)
Higher Grn. Gt G —3D **48**
Highfield Cres. Wig —5F **37**
Highfield Dri. Wig —5F **37**
Highfield Rd. Grob —2E **17**
Highfield St. Ans —5G **11**
Highfield St. Flec —5A **58**
Highfield St. Leic —3D **28**
Highfield St. Sto S —2B **50**
Highgate. Leic —4C **36**
Highgate Av. Bir —3E **13**
Highgate Dri. Leic —4D **36**
Highgrove Cres. Leic —4F **35**
Highland Av. Leic F —5E **25**
High Leys Dri. Oad —5A **38**
Highmeres Rd. Leic —2H **21**
High St. Enderby, End —6H **33**
High St. Evington, Evi —5B **30**
High St. Fleckney, Flec —5B **58**
High St. Great Glen, Gt G
—3C **48**
High St. Kibworth Harcourt, Kib
—5H **59**
High St. Leicester, Leic
—1A **28** (3B **4**)
High St. Oadby, Oad —3A **38**
High St. Syston, Sys —5E **7**
High St. Whetstone, Whet
—3H **43**
Highway Rd. Leic —5G **29**
Highway Rd. Thurm —3G **14**
Hilary Cres. Grob —2D **16**
Hilders Rd. Leic —1E **27**
Hildyard Rd. Leic —4C **20**
Hillary Pl. Leic —5E **27**
Hillberry Clo. Nar —3C **42**
Hill Ct. Thurn —3F **31**
Hillcrest Av. Kib —4H **59**
Hillcrest Rd. Leic —4D **36**
Hillcroft Clo. Thurm —3D **14**
Hillcroft Rd. Leic —2G **29**
Hill Fields. Oad —5E **39**
Hill La. Count —2A **54**
Hill La. Mark —2A **8**
Hill La. Clo. Mark —1B **8**
Hill Rise. Bir —3G **13**
Hill Rise. Leic —6D **14**
Hillrise Av. Leic —1E **35**
Hillsborough Clo. Glen P
—1C **44**
Hillsborough Cres. Glen P
—1C **44**
Hillsborough Rd. Glen P
—1C **44**
Hillside. Mark —2B **8**
Hillside Av. Wig —2B **46**
Hill St. Cft —1G **51**
Hill St. Leic —1C **28** (3E **4**)
Hilltop Av. Gt G —2E **49**
Hilltop Rd. Ham —2B **22**
Hill View Dri. Cosb —2F **53**
Hill Way. Oad —5C **38**
Hinckley Rd. Des —2A **32**
Hinckley Rd. Sto S —4A **50**
Hincks Av. Scrap —5F **23**
Hind Clo. Whet —5A **44**

Hindoostan Av. Wig —1E **45**
Hipwell Cres. Leic —2A **20**
Hoball Clo. Leic —5C **18**
Hobart St. Leic —2D **28**
Hobby Clo. B Ast —6A **52**
Hobill Clo. Hunc —3A **42**
Hobill Clo. Leic F —5H **25**
Hobrook Rd. Flec —6C **58**
Hobson Rd. Leic —2A **20**
Hoby St. Leic —1H **27**
Hockley Farm Rd. Leic —3B **26**
Hodgson Clo. Leic —4E **19**
Hodson Clo. Whet —5H **43**
Hogarth Rd. Leic —2C **12**
Holbeck Dri. B Ast —1C **60**
Holbrook. Oad —4E **39**
Holbrook Rd. Leic —2G **37**
Holden Clo. Whet —6A **44**
Holden St. Leic —3C **20**
(in three parts)
Holderness Rd. Leic —6C **12**
Holgate Clo. Ans —4G **11**
Holkham Av. Leic —4F **21**
Holland Rd. Leic —1D **28**
Holland Way. Nar —3D **42**
Holliers Way. Cft —1G **51**
Hollies Clo. Thurl —6A **32**
Hollies Way. Thurn —3F **31**
Hollington Rd. Leic —3F **29**
Hollins Rd. Leic —3C **26**
Hollinwell Clo. Leic —2A **26**
Hollow Rd. Ans —5F **11**
Hollow, The. Evi —5B **30**
Hollowtree Rd. Ham —3C **22**
Hollybank Ct. Leic —4E **29**
Hollybrook Clo. Thurm —5E **15**
Hollybush Clo. Leic —6D **22**
Hollybush Clo. Sys —5D **6**
Holly Gro. Blab —3B **44**
Holly Tree Av. Bir —3G **13**
Holmdale Rd. Sys —6E **7**
Holmden Av. Wig —1H **45**
Holme Dri. Oad —2B **38**
Holmes Clo. Grob —2E **17**
Holmewood Dri. Kir M —2F **25**
Holmfield Av. Leic —5F **29**
Holmfield Av. E. Leic —4A **26**
Holmfield Av. W. Leic F
—4H **25**
Holmfield Rd. Leic —5E **29**
Holmleigh Gdns. Thurn —3F **31**
Holmrook Ho. Leic —6G **35**
Holmwood Dri. Leic —4C **18**
Holt Cres. Thurl —6A **32**
Holt Dri. Kir M —3F **25**
Holt La. Cosb & Ash M —1H **61**
Holt Rd. Bir —6G **13**
Holts Clo. Leic —5F **35**
Holy Bones. Leic —1A **28** (3A **4**)
Holyoake St. End —1D **42**
Holyrood Dri. Count —1D **54**
Holywell Rd. Leic —3G **35**
Home Clo. Blab —3B **44**
Home Clo. Kib —5A **62**
Home Farm Clo. Leic —2G **19**
Home Farm Sq. Leic —2G **19**
Home Farm Wlk. Leic —2G **19**
Homemead Av. Leic —3H **19**
Homer Dri. Nar —3C **42**

Homestead Clo. Costn —1B **6**
Homestead Dri. Wig —2B **46**
Homestone Gdns. Leic —1E **31**
Homestone Rise. Leic —1E **31**
Homeway Rd. Leic —4G **29**
Honeybourne Clo. Oad —5A **38**
Honeycomb Clo. Nar —3C **42**
Honeysuckle Rd. Ham —3C **22**
Honiton Clo. Wig —2A **46**
Hopefield Rd. Leic —5G **27**
Hoppner Clo. Leic —2D **12**
Hopwood Clo. Leic —2F **19**
Hopyard Clo. Leic —5F **35**
Hornbeam Clo. Nar —3C **42**
Horndean Av. Wig —6E **37**
Horsefair St. Leic
—2B **28** (4C **4**)
Horsewell La. Wig —3B **46**
Horston Rd. Leic —4G **29**
Horwood Clo. Wig —5G **37**
Hoskins Clo. Wig —3C **46**
Hospital Clo. Leic —3H **29**
Hospital La. Blab —4C **44**
Hotel St. Leic —2B **28** (4C **4**)
(in two parts)
Hotoft Rd. Leic —5B **22**
Houghton La. Stoug —6F **31**
Houghton St. Leic —6F **21**
Houlditch Rd. Leic —1C **36**
Housman Wlk. Leic —5D **20**
Howard Rd. Glen P —1B **44**
Howard Rd. Leic —6C **28**
Howden Rd. Leic —5G **35**
Howdon Rd. Oad —6B **38**
Howe Clo. Sto S —4A **50**
Hoylake Clo. Leic —5G **29**
Hubbard Clo. Whet —6A **44**
Hudson Clo. Leic —5E **19**
Huggett Clo. Leic —1G **21**
Hughenden Dri. Leic —6A **28**
Humber Clo. Leic —4B **22**
Humberstone Ct. Leic —5B **22**
Humberstone Dri. Leic —6H **21**
Humberstone Ga. Leic
—1B **28** (3D **4**)
Humberstone La. Thurm
—5B **14**
Humberstone Rd. Leic
—1C **28** (3E **4**)
Humble La. Costn —1B **6**
Humes Clo. Whet —1H **53**
Humphries Clo. Leic —2A **30**
Huncote Rd. Cft —5F **41**
Huncote Rd. Hunc & Nar
—4A **42**
Huncote Rd. Sto S —2B **50**
Hungarton Boulevd. Leic
—4C **22**
Hungarton Dri. Sys —6G **7**
Hunter Rd. Leic —4C **20**
Hunters Way. Leic F —5F **25**
Hunters Way. Oad —5D **38**
Huntingdon Rd. Leic —3G **21**
Huntings, The. Kir M —2C **24**
Huntsman Clo. Mark —3C **8**
Huntsman's Dale. F Gos —1H **7**
Huntsmans Way. Leic —2F **21**
Hurds Clo. Ans —6F **11**
Hursley Clo. Oad —4C **38**

Hurst Rise. Leic —2A **30**
Hutchinson St. Leic —2D **28**
Hutchinson Wlk. Leic —2D **28**
Hyde Clo. Nar —3D **42**
Hyde Clo. Oad —6C **38**
Hydra Wlk. Leic —2D **28**
Hylion Rd. Leic —3C **36**

Ibbetson Av. Glen —6A **18**
Ibsley Way. Leic —6H **35**
Ickworth Clo. Leic —5G **21**
Iffley Clo. Leic —1H **29**
Iffley Ct. Leic —1A **30**
Iliffe Av. Oad —4H **37**
Iliffe Rd. Leic —4G **21**
Illingworth Rd. Leic —1A **30**
Ilmington Clo. Glen —4A **18**
Imperial Av. Leic —4F **27**
Imperial Rd. Kib —5H **59**
Infirmary Clo. Leic
　—3B **28** (7C **5**)
Infirmary Rd. Leic
　—3B **28** (7C **5**)
Infirmary Sq. Leic
　—3B **28** (6C **5**)
Ingarsby Dri. Leic —4C **30**
Ingleby Rd. Wig —6E **37**
Ingle Dri. Rat —5C **16**
Inglenook Pk. Thurm —2D **14**
Ingle St. Leic —6F **19**
Ingold Av. Leic —2H **19**
Ingrams Way. Wig —3C **46**
Invergarry Clo. Leic —1F **21**
Iona Clo. Leic —2F **19**
Iona Rd. Sys —5D **6**
Iona Way. Count —2F **55**
　(in two parts)
Ipswich Clo. Leic —5A **12**
Irene Pollard Ho. Leic —2D **20**
Ireton Av. Leic —3H **21**
Ireton Rd. Leic —4G **21**
Iris Av. Bir —3H **13**
Iris Av. Glen P —6F **35**
Irlam St. Wig —3F **45**
Ironworks Rd. Leic —5E **21**
Isis Clo. Oad —3D **38**
Islington St. Leic —5B **28**
Ivanhoe Clo. Glen —6A **18**
Ivanhoe Rd. Wig —1F **45**
Ivanhoe St. Leic —1G **27**
Ivatt Clo. Thurn —2G **31**
Ivychurch Cres. Leic —4D **22**
Ivydale Clo. Thurm —4D **14**
Ivydale Rd. Thurm —5D **14**
Ivy Rd. Leic —4G **27**

Jacklin Dri. Leic —6B **14**
Jackson Clo. Oad —4E **39**
Jackson St. Leic —3D **20**
Jacob Clo. End —6G **33**
Jacqueline Rd. Mark —3D **8**
Jacques Clo. End —6G **33**
James Gavin Way. Oad —5E **39**
James St. Ans —4F **11**
James St. Blab —3A **44**
James St. Sto S —2B **50**
Jamesway. Cosb —1F **53**

James Way. Mark —3C **8**
James Went Building. Leic
　—5B **5**
Jarrett Clo. End —6G **33**
Jarrom St. Leic —3A **28** (7A **5**)
Jarvis St. Leic —1A **28** (3A **4**)
Jasmine Clo. Ham —2B **22**
Jasmine Ct. Nar —2B **42**
Jasmine Ct. Wig —2F **45**
Jean Dri. Leic —4H **19**
Jellicoe Rd. Leic —1G **29**
Jennett Clo. Leic —1C **30**
Jeremy Clo. Leic —3D **20**
Jermyn St. Leic —3D **20**
Jersey Rd. Leic —6D **12**
Jessons Clo. Leic —2F **21**
Jessop Clo. Leic —5E **19**
Jetty, The. Leic —4C **4**
John Bold Av. Sto S —2C **50**
Johns Ct. Blab —3B **44**
Johnson Clo. B Ast —2C **60**
Johnson Clo. Whet —4A **44**
Johnson Rise. Sto S —4C **50**
Johnson Rd. Bir —4F **13**
Johnson St. Leic
　—6A **20** (1A **4**)
John St. End —1D **42**
Jonathan Dri. Grob —2G **17**
Jordan Av. Wig —2G **45**
Jordan Clo. Glen —5A **18**
Jordon Ct. Rat —5D **16**
Journeymans Grn. Rat —5D **16**
Jowett Clo. Leic —4E **19**
Joyce Rd. Leic —5F **19**
Jubilee Cres. Nar —4E **43**
Jubilee Dri. Glen —6A **18**
Jubilee Ho. Kir M —2D **24**
Jubilee Rd. B Ast —1A **60**
Jubilee Rd. Leic
　—6B **20** (1D **4**)
Judith Dri. Count —1F **55**
Judith Dri. Blab —3B **30**
Julian Rd. Leic —1C **44**
Junction Rd. Leic —6C **20**
Junction Rd. Wig —6F **37**
June Av. Leic —6D **14**
Junior St. Leic —1A **28** (2B **4**)
Juniper Clo. Leic F —5F **25**
Juno Clo. Glen —6A **18**
Jupiter Clo. Leic —1D **28**

Kamloops Cres. Leic
　—6C **20** (1E **4**)
Kashmir Rd. Leic —6D **20**
Kate St. Leic —2H **27**
Kay Rd. Leic —5D **18**
Keats Clo. End —6G **33**
Keats Wlk. Leic —5D **20**
Keays Way. Scrap —5F **23**
Keble Dri. Sys —6F **7**
Keble Rd. Leic —6C **28**
Kedleston Av. Bir —6G **13**
Kedleston Rd. Leic —4F **29**
Keenan Clo. Leic —4F **35**
Keepers' Croft. E Gos —2H **7**
Keepers Wlk. Leic —2F **19**
　(in two parts)
Keep, The. Kir M —2D **24**

Kegworth Av. Leic —2H **29**
Keightley Rd. Leic —4C **18**
　(in two parts)
Keightley Wlk. Thurm —5D **14**
Kelbrook Clo. Leic —1G **19**
Kelmarsh Av. Wig —1B **46**
Kelson Grn. Leic —6H **35**
Kelvon Clo. Glen —4B **18**
Kemp Rd. Leic —4C **18**
　(in two parts)
Kempson Rd. Leic —1A **36**
Kendal Clt. Leic —4A **28**
Kendall's Av. Cft —1G **51**
Kendal Rd. Leic —2F **21**
Kendrick Dri. Oad —4B **38**
Kenilworth Clo. B Ast —5A **52**
Kenilworth Dri. Oad —4H **37**
Kenilworth Rd. Wig —6B **36**
Kennedy Way. Leic F —5H **25**
Kenneth Gamble Ct. Wig
　—5D **36**
Kenny Clo. Whet —5A **44**
Kensington Clo. Glen P —2D **44**
Kensington Clo. Oad —6C **38**
Kensington Dri. Wig —4F **37**
Kensington St. Leic —4C **20**
Kent Cres. Wig —6B **36**
Kent Dri. Oad —4C **38**
Kenton Av. Wig —2A **46**
Kent St. Leic —1D **28**
Kenwood Rd. Leic —2E **37**
Kepstow Clo. Leic —5H **35**
Kerrial Gdns. Leic —6C **18**
Kerrial Rd. Leic —6C **18**
Kerrysdale Av. Leic —3F **21**
Kestrel Clo. B Ast —6A **52**
Kestrel Clo. Leic —6E **21**
Kestrel Clo. Leic F —5E **25**
Kestrel Clo. Sys —5D **6**
Keswick Clo. Bir —3H **13**
Keswick Rd. Blab —4A **44**
Kevern Clo. Wig —2B **46**
Kew Dri. Oad —6C **38**
Kew Dri. Wig —4D **36**
Keyham Clo. Leic —6D **8**
Keyham La. Leic —4A **22**
　(in two parts)
Keyham La. Scrap —1H **23**
Keyham La. E. Scrap —3H **23**
Keyham La. W. Leic —4D **22**
Keythorpe St. Leic —1D **28**
Kibworth Ct. Kib —6A **62**
Kibworth Rd. Flec **58**
Kibworth Rd. Kib —1C **62**
　(Carlton Rd.)
Kibworth Rd. Kib —4C **62**
　(Langton Rd.)
Kibworth Rd. Sad —6E **59**
Kielder Clo. Nar —1B **42**
Kilburn Av. Leic —3H **37**
Kilby Av. Bir —6G **13**
Kilby Dri. Wig —2C **46**
Kilby Rd. Flec —5G **57**
Kildare St. Leic —1B **28** (3D **4**)
Kilmelford Clo. Leic —1F **21**
Kiln Av. Thurm —5D **14**
Kiln Clo. B Ast —2C **60**
Kilverstone Av. Leic —4D **30**
Kilworth Dri. Leic —4G **29**

Kimberley Rd. Leic —4E **29**
Kimberley St. Kib —5H **59**
Kincaple Rd. Leic —1F **21**
Kincraig Rd. Leic —1F **21**
Kinder Clo. Whet —6A **44**
Kingcup Clo. Leic F —5F **25**
King Edward Av. Nar —4D **42**
King Edward Rd. Leic —6H **21**
Kingfisher Av. Leic —6E **21**
Kingfisher Clo. Gt G —2D **48**
Kingfisher Clo. Leic F —5E **25**
Kingfisher Clo. Sys —5D **6**
Kingfisher Wlk. Leic —6E **21**
King Richards Rd. Leic —2G **27**
Kingsbridge Clo. Nar —3C **42**
Kingsbridge Cres. Leic —4B **12**
Kingsbury Av. Leic —3C **30**
Kingscliffe Cres. Leic —3D **30**
Kings Dri. Leic F —5G **25**
King's Dri. Wig —6E **37**
Kingsfield Rd. Cosb —3E **53**
Kingsgate Av. Bir —3F **13**
Kingsley Clo. Nar —2C **42**
Kingsley St. Leic —1C **36**
Kings Lock Clo. Leic —5F **35**
Kingsmead Clo. Leic —3E **37**
Kingsmead Rd. Leic —2E **37**
Kings Newton St. Leic —3E **29**
Kingsthorpe Clo. Leic —2B **20**
Kingston Av. Wig —5D **36**
Kingston Rd. Leic —4E **29**
King St. Bark —4H **15**
King St. End —6H **33**
King St. Leic —2B **28** (5D **5**)
King St. Oad —4B **38**
King St. Whet —4H **43**
Kings Wlk. Leic F —4G **25**
Kings Way. Grob —3E **17**
Kingsway. Leic —1D **34**
Kingsway N. Leic —5C **26**
Kingsway Rd. Leic —5G **29**
Kingswood Av. Leic —3F **27**
Kingswood Ct. Wig —1A **46**
King Williams Way. Ans
　—4G **11**
Kinley Rd. Leic —1A **20**
Kinross Av. Leic —1E **31**
Kinsdale Dri. Leic —6E **23**
Kintyre Dri. Leic —1E **21**
Kipling Dri. Nar —1C **42**
Kipling Gro. Leic —3E **19**
Kirby Clo. Sap —5B **50**
Kirby La. Leic F —4F **25**
Kirby Rd. Glen —6F **17**
Kirby Rd. Leic —2G **27**
Kirkdale Rd. Wig —1F **45**
Kirke Wlk. Leic —1B **26**
Kirkfield Rd. Count —1F **55**
Kirkland Rd. Leic —1D **34**
Kirk La. Leic —6A **34**
Kirkscroft Wlk. Leic —2B **20**
Kirkstead Wlk. Leic —2A **20**
Kirkstone Clo. Glen —4B **18**
Kirkwall Cres. Leic —6E **23**
Kirloe Av. Leic F —4F **25**
Kirminton Gdns. Leic —1C **30**
Kirtley Way. B Ast —1C **60**
Kitchener Rd. Ans —4G **11**
Kitchener Rd. Leic —6G **21**

Kite Clo. B Ast —5A **52**
Knighton Chu. Rd. Leic —2E **37**
Knighton Clo. B Ast —3C **60**
Knighton Ct. Leic —5E **29**
Knighton Dri. Leic —1E **37**
Knighton Fields Rd. E. Leic
—1C **36**
Knighton Fields Rd. W. Leic
—1B **36**
Knighton Grange Rd. Leic
—1G **37**
Knighton Hall. Leic —1E **37**
Knighton Junc. La. Leic —6C **28**
Knighton La. Leic —1A **36**
Knighton La. E. Leic —1B **36**
Knighton Lodge. Leic —1E **37**
Knighton Pk. Rd. Leic —5D **28**
Knighton Rise. Leic —6G **29**
Knighton Rd. Leic —1D **36**
Knighton St. Leic
—3B **28** (8C **5**)
Knightsbridge Rd. Glen P
—2D **44**
Knights Clo. Sto S —3C **60**
Knights Clo. Thurm —4D **14**
Knight's Rd. Leic —5C **12**
Knollgate Clo. Bir —3E **13**
Knowles Rd. Leic —6C **18**
Knowle, The. Leic —1E **37**
Krefeld Way. Leic —2E **19**

Labrador Clo. Leic
—6C **20** (1F **4**)
Laburnum Rd. Leic —4C **22**
Ladbroke Gro. Count —1F **55**
Lady Leys. Cosb —2E **53**
Ladysmith Rd. Kir M —2D **24**
Ladysmith Rd. Wig —6A **36**
Laithwaite Clo. Leic —5B **12**
Lakeside Ct. Thurn —3E **31**
Lambert Rd. Leic —5G **27**
Lambourne Rd. Bir —3H **13**
Lamen Rd. Leic —4C **18**
Lamport Clo. Wig —1D **46**
Lancashire St. Leic —2D **20**
Lancaster Ct. Grob —3E **17**
Lancaster Pl. Leic
—4C **28** (8E **5**)
Lancaster Rd. Leic
(in two parts) —3B **28** (7D **5**)
Lancaster St. Leic —1F **29**
Lancaster Way. Glen P —2E **45**
Lancing Av. Leic —1E **27**
Landscape Dri. Leic —3C **30**
Landseer Rd. Leic —6D **28**
Lane Clo. Glen —5A **18**
Lanesborough Rd. Leic
—1D **20**
Lanes Hill Gro. Sto S —4C **50**
Langdale. Flec —5B **58**
Langdale Ho. Leic —6G **35**
Langdale Rd. Thurm —4D **14**
Langham Drl. Nar —3D **42**
Langham Rd. Leic —2H **21**
Langhill, The. Leic —1H **29**
(in two parts)
Langholm Rd. Leic —1E **31**

Langley Av. Leic —2B **20**
Langley Clo. Hunc —3A **42**
Langley Wlk. Leic —2A **20**
Langton Rd. Kib —4B **62**
Langton Rd. Wig —2B **46**
Langton St. Leic
—1B **28** (2D **4**)
Lansdowne Gro. Wig —3G **45**
Lansdowne Rd. Leic —1A **36**
Lapwing Clo. Leic —5B **12**
Lapwing Ct. Nar —4C **42**
Larch Gro. Leic —4A **26**
Larch St. Leic —6E **21**
Larchwood. Count —1E **55**
Larchwood Av. Grob —3E **17**
Larchwood Clo. Leic —2C **36**
Lark Clo. Leic F —5F **25**
Larkswood. Kib —5B **62**
Lastingham Clo. Leic —3C **36**
Latimer Clo. Blab —5A **44**
Latimer Ct. Ans —6F **11**
Latimer Pl. Leic —5C **20**
Latimer Rd. Crop —1H **11**
Latimer St. Ans —6G **11**
Latimer St. Leic —3H **27**
Launceston Ho. Wig —3A **46**
Launceston Rd. Wig —2A **46**
Launde. Mark —3D **8**
Launde Rd. Oad —2C **38**
Laundon Clo. Grob —3F **17**
Laundon Way. Grob —3E **17**
Laundon Way. Whet —6A **44**
Laundry La. Leic —2D **20**
Laurel Clo. Glen —5C **18**
Laurel Dri. Count —1E **55**
Laurel Dri. Oad —6D **38**
Laurel Rd. Blab —3B **44**
Laurel Rd. Leic —3E **29**
Laureston Dri. Leic —5F **29**
Lavender Clo. Blab —3A **44**
Lavender Rd. Leic —4G **27**
Laverstock Rd. Wig —3A **46**
Lawford Rd. Leic —5G **35**
Lawn Av. Bir —4H **13**
Lawn Clo. Thurm —4D **14**
Lawns, The. Leic —5E **29**
Lawnwood Rd. Grob —2D **16**
Lawrence Clo. Leic —2C **12**
Lawrence Kershaw Hall. Leic
—3A **28** (7B **5**)
Lawrence Wlk. Leic —2E **27**
Law St. Leic —4C **20**
Lawyers La. Oad —4A **38**
(in two parts)
Laxford Clo. Leic —3G **19**
Laxton Clo. Bir —3H **13**
Laxton Clo. Wig —1D **46**
Layton Rd. Leic —6G **21**
Lea Clo. B Ast —2C **60**
Lea Clo. Thurm —4B **14**
Leamington Dri. Blab —5B **44**
Leas Clo. Thurn —1F **31**
Lea, The. Kib —5A **62**
Ledbury Clo. Oad —5D **38**
Ledbury Grn. Leic —6D **12**
Ledwell Dri. Glen —4A **18**
Lee Circ. Leic —1C **28** (2E **4**)
Lee Rise. Rat —5D **16**
Leeson St. Leic —2A **36**

Lee St. Leic —1B **28** (2D **4**)
Legion Way. Braun —1B **34**
Leicester Airport. Leic —2H **39**
Leicester La. Des —6A **24**
Leicester La. End —6H **33**
Leicester Rd. Ans —5G **11**
Leicester Rd. Blab & Glen P
—2B **44**
Leicester Rd. B Ast —4H **51**
(in two parts)
Leicester Rd. Count —1F **55**
Leicester Rd. Flec —4B **58**
Leicester Rd. Glen —3B **18**
Leicester Rd. Grob —2F **17**
Leicester Rd. Kib —1G **59**
Leicester Rd. Mark —2C **8**
Leicester Rd. Nar —4E **43**
(in two parts)
Leicester Rd. Oad —2G **37**
Leicester Rd. Sap —6B **50**
Leicester Rd. Thurc —1B **12**
Leicester Rd. Wig —4E **37**
Leicester St. Leic —1F **29**
Leicester Western By-Pass. Leic
—5F **17**
Leire La. B Ast —3A **60**
Leire La. Leir —6D **60**
Leire Rd. Leir —6A **60**
Leire St. Leic —3D **20**
Lema Clo. Leic —6C **14**
Lena Dri. Grob —6G **9**
Leopold Clo. Count —1D **54**
Leopold Rd. Leic —6C **28**
Leopold St. Wig —2F **45**
Letchworth Rd. Leic —1E **27**
Lethbridge Clo. Leic
—6C **20** (1F **4**)
Leveret Dri. Whet —5H **43**
Leveric Rd. Leic —5G **21**
Lewis Clo. Leic —3F **19**
Lewisher Rd. Leic —2G **21**
Lewis Way. Count —2F **55**
Lewitt Clo. Leic —1H **19**
Lexham St. Leic —3D **20**
Leybury Way. Scrap —1F **31**
Leycroft Rd. Leic —5B **12**
Leyland Rd. Leic —2D **34**
Leys Clo. Oad —3C **38**
Leysdale Clo. Leic —2F **19**
Leysland Av. Count —1C **54**
Leys, The. Count —2C **54**
Leys, The. E Gos —1H **7**
Leys, The. Kib —4A **62**
Liberty Rd. Leic —1B **26**
Lichfield Av. B Ast —5H **51**
Lichfield Dri. Blab —5B **44**
Lichfield St. Leic
—6B **20** (1C **4**)
Lidster Clo. Leic —5B **22**
Lilac Av. Leic —4C **22**
Lilac Wlk. Leic —4C **22**
Lillington Clo. Mark —2C **8**
Limber Cres. Leic —4C **26**
Lime Av. Grob —3E **17**
Lime Clo. Sys —6F **17**
Lime Dri. Sys —1F **15**
Lime Gro. Blab —3B **44**
Lime Gro. Kir M —2D **24**
Lime Gro. Clo. Leic —1G **19**

Limehurst Rd. Leic —4D **22**
Lime Kilns. Wig —3C **46**
Lime Tree Av. Bir —3G **13**
Limetree Rd. Nar —1F **43**
Linacres Rd. Leic —4C **26**
Lincoln Dri. Blab —5B **44**
Lincoln Dri. Sys —1G **15**
Lincoln Dri. Wig —1F **45**
Lincoln St. Leic —2D **28**
Linden Av. Count —1C **54**
Linden Dri. Leic —4H **29**
Linden Farm Dri. Count
—1D **54**
Linden La. Kir M —3F **25**
Linden St. Leic —2F **29**
Lindfield Rd. Leic —6E **19**
Lindisfarne Rd. Sys —6D **6**
Lindrick Dri. Leic —5G **29**
Lindsay Rd. Leic —6F **27**
Lindum Clo. Sys —1D **14**
Linford Clo. Wig —1C **46**
Linford Cres. Mark —3C **8**
Linford St. Leic —2C **20**
Ling Dale. E Gos —2H **7**
Lingdale Lodge. E Gos —2H **7**
Link Rise. Mark —3D **8**
Link Rd. Ans —5E **11**
Link Rd. Leic —2G **37**
Link Rd. Quen —4H **7**
Links Rd. Kib —5B **62**
Links Rd. Kir M —3C **24**
Linkway Gdns. Leic —2G **27**
Linley Grn. Cosb —2F **53**
Linnet Clo. Nar —4C **42**
Linney Rd. Leic —3G **19**
Lintlaw Clo. Leic —1F **21**
Linton St. Leic —3E **29**
Linwood La. Leic —3B **36**
Lipton Rd. Leic —5B **12**
Lismore Wlk. Leic —2F **19**
Litelmede. Leic —6G **21**
Little Av. Leic —2C **20**
Lit. Barley Clo. Leic —2F **19**
Lit. Dale. Wig —2C **46**
Littlefare, The. Leic —5B **26**
Littlegarth. Leic —4B **36**
Lit. Glen Rd. Glen P —1B **44**
Little Hill. Wig —1B **46**
Lit. Holme St. Leic —2H **27**
Lit. John Rd. Leic —5H **35**
Little La. Leic —6B **60**
Lit. Lunnon. Dun B —6E **61**
Lit. Markfield. Mark —3A **8**
Lit. Masons Clo. Leic —6A **26**
Lit. Meer Clo. Braun —6B **26**
Littlemore Clo. Leic —1H **29**
Littleton St. Leic —6H **19**
Littleway, The. Leic —1H **29**
(in two parts)
Lit. Wood Clo. Leic —1G **19**
Livesey Dri. Sap —6A **50**
Livingstone St. Leic —3G **27**
Llewellyn Ct. Leic —6F **29**
Lobbs Wood Clo. Leic —5B **22**
Lobelia Clo. Nar —3B **42**
Locke Av. Leic —6B **14**
Lockerbie Av. Leic —1E **21**
Lockerbie Wlk. Leic —1F **21**
Lockhouse Clo. Leic —5F **35**

Lodge Clo. Hunc —3H **41**
Lodge Clo. Kib —3H **59**
Lodge Clo. Sys —5G **7**
Lodge Clo. Thurm —5D **14**
Lodge Farm Rd. Leic —1C **30**
Lodge M. Leic —3E **31**
Lodgewood Av. Bir —4F **13**
Logan Av. Leic —3G **35**
Lombardy Rise. Leic —6E **21**
Lomond Cres. Leic —3G **19**
London Rd. Leic
—3C **28** (6F **5**)
London Rd. Mark —3B **8**
London Rd. Oad & Gt G
—4B **38**
London Rd. Oad —1A **48**
London St. Leic —1F **29**
Longcliffe Rd. Leic —6E **21**
Longfellow Rd. Leic —1C **36**
Longford Clo. Wig —3A **46**
Long Furrow. E Gos —2H **7**
Longhade Furlong. Ans —4H **11**
Longhurst Clo. Leic —6C **14**
Long La. Leic —1A **28** (2B **4**)
Long La. Wig —1B **46**
Longleat Clo. Leic —5F **21**
Long Meadow. Wig —3C **46**
Longrey. Flec —4A **58**
Longstone Grn. Leic —6E **23**
Long St. Sto S —2C **60**
Long St. Wig —1A **46**
Lonsdale Rd. Thurm —5C **14**
Lonsdale St. Leic —3E **29**
Lord Byron St. Leic —1C **36**
Lords Av. Leic —4C **12**
Lorne Rd. Leic —6C **28**
Lorraine Rd. Leic —2H **35**
Lorrimer Rd. Leic —1A **36**
Loseby La. Leic —2B **28** (4C **4**)
Lothair Rd. Leic —6A **28**
Loughborough Rd. Leic & Bir
—1C **20**
Louise Av. Grob —3F **17**
Lound Rd. Sap —5B **50**
Lovelace Way. Flec —6C **58**
Loves La. Dun B —6F **61**
Lowcroft Dri. Oad —5C **38**
Lwr. Brown St. Leic
—3B **28** (6C **5**)
Lwr. Church St. Sys —5F **7**
Lwr. Free La. Leic
—1B **28** (3D **4**)
Lwr. Hastings St. Leic
—3C **28** (7E **5**)
Lwr. Hill St. Leic —1B **28** (2D **4**)
Lwr. Lee St. Leic —1B **28** (2D **4**)
Lwr. Willow St. Leic —6C **20**
Lowick Dri. Wig —1C **46**
Lowland Av. Leic F —5G **25**
Loxley Rd. Glen —4A **18**
Lubbesthorpe Bridle Rd. Leic
—6C **26**
Lubbesthorpe Rd. Leic —2C **34**
Lubbesthorpe Way. Leic
—5B **26**
Ludgate Clo. Bir —3E **13**
Ludlam Clo. Count —1C **54**
Ludlow Clo. Oad —4C **38**
Lulworth Clo. Leic —3H **29**

Lulworth Clo. Wig —4B **46**
Lunsford Rd. Leic —5F **21**
Luther St. Leic —3G **27**
Lutterworth Rd. Count & Blab
—3A **54**
Lutterworth Rd. Dun B & Cosb
—6G **61**
Lutterworth Rd. Leic —5G **35**
Lydall Rd. Leic —5A **36**
Lydford Rd. Leic —3G **21**
Lyle Clo. Leic —6C **14**
Lyme Rd. Leic —4E **29**
Lymington Rd. Leic —5D **22**
Lyncote Rd. Leic —1F **35**
Lyndale Clo. Thurm —5C **14**
Lyndale Rd. Leic —1D **34**
Lyndhurst. Leic —5E **29**
Lyndhurst Rd. Oad —3A **38**
Lyndon Dri. Oad —3H **37**
Lyndwood Ct. Leic —6F **29**
Lyngate Av. Bir —3G **13**
Lynholme Rd. Leic —3D **36**
Lynmouth Clo. Glen —6A **18**
Lynmouth Dri. Wig —4C **36**
Lynmouth Rd. Leic —5D **22**
Lyon Clo. Wig —5C **36**
Lytham Rd. Leic —6C **28**
Lytton Rd. Leic —5D **28**
(in two parts)

Mablowe Field. Wig —3C **46**
MacAuley St. Leic —1B **36**
MacDonald Rd. Leic —4C **20**
McKenzie Wlk. Leic —2A **30**
Mackenzie Way. Leic
—6C **20** (1F **4**)
McVicker Clo. Leic —1A **30**
Madeline Rd. Leic —5C **12**
Madras Rd. Leic —1D **28**
Magazine Wlk. Leic
—2A **28** (5B **5**)
Magna Rd. Wig —2G **45**
Magna Rd. Ind. Est. Wig
—2G **45**
Magnolia Clo. Leic —4G **35**
Magnolia Clo. Leic F —5E **25**
Magnus Rd. Leic —3E **21**
Maiden St. Sys —6D **6**
Maidenwell Av. Ham —4C **22**
Maidstone Rd. Leic —2D **28**
Maidwell Clo. Wig —1D **46**
Mains La. Bur O —5F **49**
Main St. Bark —3G **15**
Main St. B Ast —6A **52**
Main St. Bur O —3H **49**
Main St. Cosb —2F **53**
Main St. Costn —1A **6**
Main St. Count —2F **55**
Main St. Dun B —5F **61**
Main St. Evi —5B **30**
Main St. Flec —6A **58**
Main St. Glen —5H **17**
Main St. Hum —5A **22**
Main St. Hunc —4H **41**
Main St. Kib —3A **62**
Main St. Kilb —2D **56**
Main St. Kir M —2D **24**
Main St. Leic —5C **26**

Main St. Leir —6A **60**
Main St. Mark —3B **8**
Main St. New L —2H **9**
Main St. Rat —5C **16**
Main St. Scrap —5F **23**
Main St. Sm W —6H **59**
Main St. Thurl —6A **32**
Main St. Thurn —3F **31**
Malabar Rd. Leic —6D **20**
Malcolm Arc. Leic —3C **4**
Malham Clo. Leic —2G **19**
Malham Way. Oad —4D **38**
Mallard Av. Grob —2E **17**
Mallard Dri. Sys —5D **6**
Mallard Way. Leic F —5E **25**
Malling Av. B Ast —6H **51**
Malling Clo. Bir —2H **13**
Mallory Pl. Leic —5G **21**
Mallow Clo. Ham —2C **22**
Malton Dri. Oad —3C **38**
Malvern Cres. Cosb —2F **53**
Malvern Rd. Leic —5F **29**
Mandarin Way. Whet —1H **53**
Mandervell Rd. Oad —4H **37**
Mandora La. Leic —3D **28**
Manitoba Rd. Leic
—6C **20** (1E **4**)
Mann Clo. Braun —5B **26**
Manners Rd. Leic —2A **36**
Manor Brook Clo. Sto S
—2C **50**
Manor Clo. Oad —1B **38**
Manor Ct. Blab —3C **44**
Manor Dri. Leic —6A **12**
Manor Farm Clo. B Ast —1B **60**
Manor Farm Way. Glen —6A **18**
Manor Gdns. Glen —5A **18**
Manor Ho. Gdns. Hum —5B **22**
Manor Rd. Cosb —1F **53**
Manor Rd. Flec —6C **58**
Manor Rd. Oad —1H **37**
Manor Rd. Sap —5B **50**
Manor Rd. Thurm —5B **14**
Manor Rd. Extension. Oad
—2B **38**
Manor St. Wig —1H **45**
Mansfield St. Leic
—1B **28** (2C **4**)
Manston Clo. Leic —6E **15**
Mantle Rd. Leic —1H **27**
Manton Clo. B Ast —1D **60**
Maple Av. Blab —5B **44**
Maple Av. Count —1F **55**
Maple Av. Leic —4A **26**
Maple Clo. Leic —3A **20**
Maple Rd. Thurm —5B **14**
Mapleton Rd. Wig —6E **37**
Maple Tree Wlk. L'thrpe
—4E **43**
Maplewell Dri. Leic —5A **12**
Maplin Rd. Leic —4E **23**
Marble St. Leic —2B **28** (5C **5**)
Marcus Clo. Sys —1C **14**
Marefield Clo. Thurn —1G **31**
Marfitt St. Leic —3D **20**
Margaret Anne Rd. Oad
—5B **38**
Margaret Clo. Thurm —3C **14**
Margaret Cres. Wig —6D **36**

Margaret Rd. Leic —2G **29**
(in two parts)
Marigold Way. Nar —3B **42**
Marina Dri. Grob —2G **17**
Marina Rd. Leic —3F **29**
Marjorie St. Leic —4C **20**
Market Pl. Leic —2B **28** (4C **4**)
Market Pl. App. Leic
—2B **28** (4D **4**)
Market Pl. S. Leic
—2B **28** (4C **4**)
Market St. Leic —2B **28** (4C **4**)
Markfield Ind. Est. Mark —1A **8**
Markfield La. Mark —6C **8**
Markfield La. Mark & New L
—2D **8**
Markfield La. Rat —2A **16**
Markfield Rd. Grob —1D **16**
Markfield Rd. Rat —3A **16**
Markland. Leic —5G **35**
Marlborough Dri. Flec —6C **58**
Marlborough St. Leic
—2B **28** (5D **5**)
Marlow Rd. Leic —5H **27**
Marmion Clo. Flec —6C **58**
Maromme Sq. Wig —6F **37**
Marquis St. Leic
—3B **28** (6D **5**)
Marriot Dri. Kib —5B **62**
Marriott Rd. Leic —4A **36**
Marsden Av. Quen —4H **7**
Marsden La. Leic —3F **35**
Marshall St. Leic —6H **19**
Marsh Av. Kib —4B **62**
Marsh Clo. Leic —6C **14**
Marsh Dri. Kib —4A **62**
Marston Clo. Oad —6A **38**
Marston Clo. Sto S —1C **50**
Marston Cres. Count —2E **55**
Marston Dri. Grob —2F **17**
Marston Ho. Leic —6D **20**
Marston Rd. Cft —6F **41**
Marston Rd. Leic —3G **21**
Marstown Av. Wig —1F **45**
Martin Av. Leic F —4F **25**
Martin Av. Oad —3B **38**
Martin Clo. Leic —5D **20**
Martin Clo. Sto S —4B **50**
Martindale Clo. Leic —4A **28**
Martin Dri. Sys —5C **6**
Martinshaw La. Grob —2E **17**
Martin Sq. Rat —5D **16**
Martin St. Leic —5D **20**
Martival. Leic —6G **21**
Marvin Clo. Leic —6F **19**
Marwell Clo. Leic —1B **20**
Marwell Wlk. Leic —1B **20**
Marwood Rd. Leic —1H **19**
Marydene Dri. Leic —4C **30**
Mary Gee Houses. Leic —1F **37**
Mary Rd. Leic —5F **19**
Mary's Ct. Ans —5F **11**
Masefield Av. Nar —1C **42**
Mason Clo. Nar —4D **42**
Matlock Av. Wig —2G **45**
Matlock Clo. Leic —1E **29**
Matts Clo. Leic —4H **35**
Maura Clo. Whet —6H **43**
Maurice Dri. Count —2D **54**

Mavis Av. Leic —5G **27**
Mawby Clo. Whet —6A **44**
Maxfield Ho. Leic —2D **28**
Mayfield Dri. Wig —4F **37**
Mayfield Rd. Leic —4E **29**
Mayflower Clo. Mark —3B **8**
Mayflower Ct. Mark —3C **8**
Mayflower Rd. Leic —4G **29**
Maynard Rd. Leic —1D **28**
  (in two parts)
Mayor's Wlk. Leic —4C **28**
Mays Farm Dri. Sto S —1B **50**
Maytree Clo. Leic F —4E **25**
Maytree Dri. Leic F —4E **25**
Meadhurst Rd. Leic —2E **27**
Meadowbrook Rd. Kib —5H **59**
Meadow Clo. Rat —5D **16**
Meadow Clo. Sto S —2B **50**
Meadow Ct. Leic —2G **35**
Meadow Ct. Nar —2C **42**
Meadow Ct. Rd. Grob —2F **17**
Meadowcourt Rd. Leic —2H **37**
Meadowcroft Clo. Glen —6H **17**
Meadow Gdns. Leic —3C **36**
Meadow Hill. Gt G —3C **48**
Meadow La. Bir —3H **13**
Meadow La. Mark —2C **8**
Meadow La. Sys —5B **6**
Meadows Edge. Nar —1C **42**
Meadows, The. L'thrpe —4F **43**
Meadowsweet Rd. Ham
  —3C **22**
Meadow, The. B Ast —2C **60**
Meadow View. Oad —4B **38**
Meadow Way. Grob —2F **17**
Meadow Way. Wig —1C **46**
Meads, The. Leic —2C **26**
Meadvale Rd. Leic —2D **36**
Meadway. Leic —1E **27**
Meadway, The. Bir —3G **13**
Meadway, The. Sys —1D **14**
Meadwell Rd. Leic —3B **26**
Medhurst Clo. Whet —6A **44**
Medina Rd. Leic —5H **19**
Medway St. Leic —3E **29**
Meer, The. Flec —6C **58**
Melba Way. Bir —2H **13**
Melbourne Clo. Kib —5H **59**
Melbourne Rd. Leic —2E **29**
Melbourne St. Leic —1D **28**
Melcombe Wlk. Leic —2B **20**
Melford St. Leic —6H **21**
Melland Pl. Leic —4A **36**
Mellerstain Wlk. Leic —6G **21**
Mellier Clo. Nar —1C **42**
Mellor Rd. Leic —2E **27**
Melrose St. Leic —4D **20**
Melton Av. Leic —6A **14**
Melton Dri. B Ast —5A **52**
Melton Rd. Leic & Sys —4D **20**
Melton St. Leic —6D **20**
Memory La. Leic —6C **20**
Mendip Av. Leic —4G **19**
Mennecy Clo. Count —2D **54**
Mensa Clo. Leic —2E **29**
Menzies Rd. Leic —3A **20**
Mercer's Way. E Gos —2H **7**
Merchants Comn. E Gos —2H **7**
Mercia Dri. Oad —3H **37**

Mercury Clo. Leic —2D **28**
Mere Clo. Leic —1E **29**
Meredith Rd. Leic —6F **27**
Mere Rd. Count —6E **55**
Mere Rd. Leic —6E **21**
Mere Rd. Wig —6G **37**
Meres Wlk. Wig —6H **37**
Mereworth Clo. Leic —5F **21**
Meridian Bus. Pk. Leic —3B **34**
Meridian E. Leic —1B **34**
  (in two parts)
Meridian N. Leic —2B **34**
Meridian S. Leic —3B **34**
Meridian Way. Leic —6B **26**
Meridian W. Leic —2B **34**
Merlin Clo. B Ast —6A **52**
Merlin Clo. Leic F —5G **25**
Merton Av. Leic —2G **27**
Merton Av. Sys —6F **7**
Merton Clo. B Ast —6H **51**
Merton Ho. Leic —1A **30**
Merton Way. Kib —4H **59**
Mervyn Rd. Leic —3F **29**
Metcalfe Clo. Sto S —3B **50**
Methuen Av. Thurm —3C **14**
Meynell Clo. Oad —5C **38**
Meynell Rd. Leic —6F **21**
Michael Ramsey Ct. Leic
  —6G **35**
Mickleton Dri. Leic —4B **30**
Middlefield Clo. Costn —1B **6**
Middlesex Rd. Leic —2H **35**
Middleton Clo. Sto S —3C **50**
Middleton Clo. Wig —6H **37**
Middleton St. Leic —2G **35**
Midhurst Av. Leic —1D **34**
Midland Cotts. Wig —1H **45**
Midland St. Leic —1C **28** (3F **4**)
Midway Rd. Leic —5F **29**
Milestone Clo. Kib —5B **62**
Milford Clo. Nar —3D **42**
Milford Rd. Leic —1D **36**
Millbrook Clo. Leic —2B **20**
Millbrook Dri. B Ast —2B **60**
Millbrook Wlk. Leic —2A **20**
Mill Clo. Sap —5C **50**
Mill Clo. Sm W —6H **59**
Mill Clo. Wig —3F **45**
Mill Dri. Rat —6D **16**
Miller Clo. Leic —6C **14**
Millers Clo. Glen —5G **17**
Millers Clo. Sys —6E **7**
Millersdale Av. Leic —3D **30**
Millers Grange. B Ast —2B **60**
Millfield Clo. Ans —6F **11**
Millfield Cres. Leic —3D **34**
Mill Hill. End —4G **33**
Mill Hill. Leic —3C **20**
Mill Hill Clo. Whet —4A **44**
Mill Hill Ind. Est. End —5G **33**
Mill Hill La. Leic —3D **28**
Milligan Rd. Leic —3A **36**
Mill La. Blab —3C **44**
Mill La. Earl S & Thurl —3A **40**
Mill La. End —6H **33**
Mill La. Leic —3A **28** (6A **5**)
Mill La. Sm W —6E **59**
Mill La. Sys —4D **6**
Mill La. Thurm —3B **14**

Mill La., The. Glen —5G **17**
Mill Rd. Thurc —1B **12**
Millstone La. Leic
  —2A **28** (5B **5**)
Millstone La. Sys —4G **7**
Mill St. Leic —3B **28** (6D **5**)
Mill View. Hunc —4H **41**
Millwood Clo. Leic —6E **13**
Milnroy Rd. Leic —1E **31**
Milton Clo. Wig —1C **46**
Milton Cres. Leic —2E **19**
Milton Gdns. Oad —4A **38**
Milton Ho. Leic —2F **19**
Milton St. Nar —2C **42**
Milverton Av. Leic —4G **19**
Milverton Clo. Wig —5E **37**
Milverton Dri. Wig —5E **37**
Minehead St. Leic —2F **27**
Minster Cres. Leic —4H **19**
Minstrels Wlk. E Gos —2H **7**
Mitchell Rd. End —6G **33**
Moat Clo. Thurl —6A **32**
Moat Gdns. Sap —6B **50**
Moat Rd. Leic —2F **29**
Moat St. Wig —1A **46**
Modbury Av. Leic —1A **20**
Moira St. Leic —4D **20**
Monal Clo. Whet —1H **53**
Monarch Clo. Bir —3A **14**
Monar Clo. Leic —1F **21**
Monckton Clo. Leic
  —6C **20** (1F **4**)
Monica Rd. Leic —2D **34**
Monks Cres. Leic —3C **12**
Monmouth Dri. Leic —1C **44**
Monsell Dri. Leic —4G **35**
Montague Av. Sys —1F **15**
Montague Rd. B Ast —6B **52**
Montague Rd. Leic —5D **28**
Montreal Rd. Leic —6C **20**
Montrose Ct. Leic —5A **22**
Montrose Rd. Leic —4G **35**
Montrose Rd. S. Leic —4G **35**
Moon Clo. Leic —2D **28**
Moores Clo. Wig —1E **45**
Moores La. End —6H **33**
Moores Rd. Leic —3D **20**
Moorfields. Leic —5D **22**
Moorgate Av. Bir —3F **13**
Moorgate St. Leic —5C **20**
Moorland Rd. Sys —5C **6**
Morban Rd. Leic —3F **35**
Morcote Rd. Leic —4C **26**
Morland Av. Leic —1G **37**
Morledge St. Leic
  —1C **28** (3F **4**)
Morley Arc. Leic —3D **4**
Morley Rd. Sap —6C **50**
Morley St. Leic —1E **29**
Mornington St. Leic —6F **21**
Morpeth Av. Leic —6C **12**
Morpeth Clo. Oad —5D **38**
Morris Clo. Leic —2E **19**
Morrison Ct. Kib —6A **62**
Morris Rd. Leic —6C **28**
Mortiboys Way. Sto S —3B **50**
Mortimer Pl. Leic —6F **27**
Mortimer Rd. Nar —4C **42**
Mortimer Way. Leic —6E **27**

Mortoft Rd. Leic —2D **20**
Morton Wlk. Leic —5F **21**
Morwoods, The. Oad —4B **38**
Mossdale Clo. Leic
  —4A **28** (7B **5**)
Mossdale Rd. Leic —1C **34**
Mosse Way. Oad —3C **38**
Mossgate. Leic —6E **19**
Mostyn Av. Sys —5G **7**
Mostyn St. Leic —2F **27**
Mottisford Rd. Leic —1B **20**
Mottisford Wlk. Leic —1B **20**
Mountain Rd. Leic —1A **22**
Mount Av. Leic —1F **29**
Mountcastle Rd. Leic —5G **27**
Mt. Pleasant. Oad —6E **39**
Mount Rd. Cosb —2F **53**
Mount Rd. Leic —1E **29**
Mount Rd. Oad —4B **38**
Mount, The. Dun B —6E **61**
Mount, The. Scrap —5F **23**
Mount View. Gt G —2D **48**
Mowbray Dri. Sys —5G **7**
Mowmacre Hill. Leic —6E **13**
Mowsley End. Wig —1B **46**
Muirfield Clo. Leic —2A **26**
Mulberry Av. Leic —1A **26**
Mull Way. Count —2F **55**
Mundella St. Leic —4E **29**
Municipal Sq. W. Leic —4D **4**
Munnings Clo. Leic —5D **20**
Muntjack Rd. Whet —5H **43**
Muriel Rd. Leic —2G **27**
Murrayfield Rd. Leic —2A **26**
Murray St. Leic —1D **28**
Museum Sq. Leic
  —3C **28** (6E **5**)
Musgrove Clo. Leic —2H **27**
Musson Rd. Leic —6C **18**
Myrtle Av. Bir —2H **13**
Myrtle Rd. Leic —3E **29**

Nagle Gro. Leic —6B **14**
Namur Rd. Wig —6A **36**
Nansen Rd. Leic —3G **29**
Narborough Rd. Cosb —6E **43**
Narborough Rd. Hunc —4H **41**
Narborough Rd. Leic —6F **27**
Narborough Rd. N. Leic
  —2H **27**
Narborough Rd. S. Leic —5C **34**
  (in five parts)
Narborough Wood Pk. Ind. Est.
  End —2D **32**
Narrow Boat Clo. Wig —3G **45**
Narrow La. Leic —3G **35**
Naseby Clo. Wig —1C **46**
Naseby Rd. Leic —3G **21**
Naseby Way. Gt G —3D **48**
Navigation St. Leic —6B **20**
Naylor Rd. Sys —4G **7**
Neal Av. Leic —5C **26**
Necton St. Sys —6E **7**
Nedham St. Leic —1D **28**
Needham Av. Glen P —6E **35**
Needham Clo. Oad —5E **39**
Needlegate. Leic
  —6A **20** (1B **4**)

Needwood Way. Nar —1B **42**
Nelot Way. Leic —2B **30**
Nelson St. Leic —3C **28** (6F **5**)
Nelson St. Sys —6F **7**
Nene Ct. Oad —4C **38**
Nene Dri. Oad —4C **38**
Neptune Clo. Leic —2E **29**
Neston Gdns. Leic —3B **36**
Neston Rd. Leic —3B **36**
Netherfield Rd. Ans —4G **11**
Nether Field Way. Braun
      —6B **26**
Netherhall La. Bir —5H **13**
Nether Hall Rd. Leic —5C **22**
Netton Clo. Wig —3A **46**
Nevanthon Rd. Leic —2F **27**
Neville Dri. Mark —3B **8**
Neville Rd. Leic —2F **27**
Newarke Clo. Leic
      —3A **28** (6A **5**)
Newarke Grn. Leic
      —2A **28** (5B **5**)
Newarke St. Leic —2A **28** (5C **5**)
Newarke, The. Leic
      —2A **28** (5A **5**)
Newark Rd. Thurm —2C **14**
New Bond St. Leic
      —1B **28** (3C **4**)
New Bri. Rd. Glen P —1B **44**
New Bri. St. Leic —4A **28**
Newbury Clo. Wig —2A **46**
Newby Clo. Whet —2H **43**
Newby Gdns. Oad —5E **39**
Newcombe Rd. Leic —5F **27**
New Croft Av. Leic —2F **27**
New Fields Av. Leic —5E **27**
New Fields Sq. Leic —6F **27**
New Forest Clo. Wig —3B **46**
Newgate End. Wig —1A **46**
Newham Clo. Leic —6E **15**
Newhaven Rd. Leic —4D **30**
New Henry St. Leic
      —6A **20** (1A **4**)
Newington St. Leic —3D **20**
Newington Wlk. Leic —3D **20**
New Inn Clo. B Ast —2C **60**
Newlyn Pde. Leic —4D **22**
Newmarket St. Leic —1D **36**
Newmarket Wlk. Leic —1D **36**
New Pk. Rd. Leic —1A **36**
New Parks Boulevd. Leic
(in three parts) —2B **26**
New Parks Cres. Leic —5E **19**
New Pk. St. Leic
      —2H **27** (5A **5**)
New Parks Way. Leic —2B **26**
New Parliament St. Leic
      —1B **28** (2D **4**)
New Pingle St. Leic
      —6A **20** (1A **4**)
Newpool Bank. Oad —4E **39**
Newport Pl. Leic
      —2C **28** (5E **5**)
Newport St. Leic —1G **27**
Newquay Dri. Glen —4A **18**
New Rd. Kib —5A **62**
New Rd. Leic —1B **28** (2C **4**)
New Rd. Sto S —3B **50**
New Romney Clo. Leic —5E **23**

New Romney Cres. Leic
      —5E **23**
Newry, The. Leic —4B **36**
New Star Rd. Leic —1A **22**
Newstead Av. Leic —4G **19**
Newstead Av. Wlg —5E **37**
Newstead Rd. Leic —1E **37**
Newstead Way. Leic —3G **31**
New St. Blab —3B **44**
New St. Count —1F **55**
New St. Leic —2A **28** (4C **4**)
New St. Oad —3A **38**
New St. Quen —4H **7**
New St. Sto S —1B **50**
Newton Dri. Bir —3H **13**
Newton La. Gt G —4C **48**
Newton La. Wig & New H
(in two parts) —1B **46**
Newton Way. B Ast —3B **60**
Newtown Linford La. Grob
(in two parts) —5A **10**
Newtown St. Leic
      —3B **28** (7D **5**)
New Wlk. Leic —2B **28** (5D **5**)
New Wlk. Sap —6B **50**
New Way Rd. Leic —5F **29**
New Wycliffe Home. Leic
      —2F **21**
New Zealand La. Quen —3G **7**
Nicholas Dri. Rat —5C **16**
Nichols St. Leic —1C **28** (3F **4**)
Nicklaus Rd. Leic —1F **21**
Nidderdale Rd. Wig —1D **46**
Noble St. Leic —1G **27**
Nock Verges. Sto S —3B **50**
Noel St. Leic —4H **27**
Nook Clo. Rat —4C **16**
Nook St. Leic —4C **48**
Nook, The. Ans —5G **11**
Nook, The. Cosb —3F **53**
Nook, The. End —6G **33**
Nook, The. Gt G —4C **48**
Nook, The. Mark —2B **8**
Nook, The. Whet —4H **43**
Norbury Av. Leic —4E **21**
Norfolk Rd. Wig —6B **36**
Norfolk St. Leic —2H **27**
Norfolk Wlk. Leic —2H **27**
Norman Clo. Oad —5D **38**
Normandy Clo. Glen —6A **18**
Norman Rd. Thurm —3B **14**
Norman St. Leic —3H **27**
Normanton Gro. Thurl —1E **41**
Normanton Rd. Leic —3E **29**
Northampton Sq. Leic
      —2C **28** (4E **4**)
Northampton St. Leic
      —2C **28** (5E **5**)
North Av. Leic —5E **29**
North Bri. Pl. Leic —6H **19**
Northcote Rd. Leic —1D **36**
N. Deepdale. Leic —1H **29**
Northdene Rd. Leic —4C **36**
Northdown Dri. Thurm —5C **14**
North Dri. Leic —5A **22**
N. End Clo. Leic —3B **36**
Northfield Av. Bir —3H **13**
Northfield Av. Wig —5D **36**
Northfield Rd. Blab —2B **44**

Northfield Rd. Leic —4G **21**
Northfields. Sys —5F **7**
Northfold Rd. Leic —3E **37**
Northgates. Leic
      —1A **28** (2A **4**)
Northgate St. Leic
      —6A **20** (1A **4**)
North St. Oad —3A **38**
North St. Sys —5E **7**
North St. Wig —6F **37**
Northumberland Av. Leic
      —3E **21**
Northumberland Rd. Wig
      —6B **36**
Northumberland St. Leic
      —6A **20** (1A **4**)
Norton St. Leic —3B **28** (6C **5**)
Norwich Rd. Leic —2H **19**
Norwood Rd. Leic —4G **29**
Nottingham Rd. Leic —1F **29**
Nugent St. Leic —1H **27**
Nursery Clo. Quen —4H **7**
Nursery Clo. Thurl —1E **41**
Nursery Clo. Thurm —5B **14**
Nursery Hollow. Glen P —6E **35**
Nursery Rd. Leic —6D **22**
Nutfield Rd. Leic —4G **27**
Nuthall Gro. Glen P —5F **35**

Oadby Hill Dri. Oad —3H **37**
Oadby Rd. Wig —6F **37**
Oak & Ash Bus. Pk. Leic
      —6E **21**
Oak Av. Leir —6A **60**
Oak Cres. Leic —5A **26**
Oakcroft Av. Kir M —2E **25**
Oakdale Clo. Leic —1A **26**
Oakdene Rd. Leic —3C **36**
Oak Dri. Sys —1F **15**
Oakenshaw Clo. Leic —6E **13**
Oakfield Av. B Ast —4F **13**
Oakfield Av. Glen —3B **18**
Oakfield Av. Mark —3B **8**
Oakfield Clo. Gt G —2D **48**
Oakfield Cres. Blab —5C **44**
Oakfield Rd. Leic —4E **29**
Oakland Av. Leic —6H **13**
Oakland Rd. Leic —6C **28**
Oakleigh Av. Glen P —2E **45**
Oakley Rd. Leic —6F **21**
Oakmeadow. Glen —6H **17**
Oakmeadow Way. Grob —3E **17**
Oak Pool Gdns. Leic —6H **35**
Oak Rd. L'thrpe —5E **43**
Oaks Ct. Nar —3C **42**
Oaks Dri. Blab —4C **44**
Oakside Clo. Leic —3C **30**
Oakside Cres. Leic —2C **30**
Oaks Ind. Est. Earl S —4C **42**
Oaks Rd. Gt G —3D **48**
Oak St. Leic —6E **21**
Oaks Way. Leic —1H **37**
Oakthorpe Av. Leic —3F **27**
Oaktree Clo. Grob —2E **17**
Oak Tree Clo. Ham —3C **22**
Oaktree Clo. Kib —4B **62**
Oakwood Av. Wig —5F **37**
Oakwood Clo. Leic F —5F **25**

Oasis, The. Glen —5H **17**
Oban St. Leic —1G **27**
Ocean Clo. Leic —6C **22**
Ocean Rd. Leic —1C **30**
(in four parts)
Odam Clo. Leic —5D **26**
Odeon Arc. Leic —4C **4**
Offranville Clo. Thurm —5D **14**
Ogwen Clo. Leic —1D **30**
Okehampton Av. Leic —4H **29**
Okehampton Wlk. Leic —4H **29**
Old Barn Wlk. Leic —2G **19**
Old Chu. St. Leic —3G **35**
Oldfield Clo. Count —1C **54**
Old Forge Rd. Ash M —5H **61**
Old Garden Clo. Blab —4B **44**
Old Hall Clo. Grob —3F **17**
Old Hall Clo. Thurm —3B **14**
Old Mill. B Ast —2B **60**
Old Mill La. Leic —6A **20** (1A **4**)
Old Mill Rd. B Ast —2B **60**
Old Milton St. Leic
      —6C **20** (1E **4**)
Old Rectory Clo. B Ast —1A **60**
Old Saffron La. Leic —6A **28**
Oliver Ct. Leic —6F **29**
Oliver Rd. Leic —3F **21**
Oliver St. Leic —1A **36**
Olphin St. Leic —5C **20**
Olympic Clo. Glen —5B **18**
Onslow St. Leic —3E **29**
Ontario Clo. Leic
      —6C **20** (1E **4**)
Orange St. Wig —3F **45**
Orchard Av. Glen P —6F **35**
Orchard Clo. Oad —5A **38**
Orchard Dri. Wig —1H **45**
Orchard Gdns. Thurm —5D **14**
Orchard La. Count —2F **55**
Orchard La. Gt G —4D **38**
Orchard Rd. Bir —4H **13**
Orchard Rd. B Ast —6A **52**
Orchardson Av. Leic —5C **20**
Orchard St. Flec —6B **58**
Orchard St. Leic
      —6B **20** (1D **4**)
Orchard, The. Grob —2E **17**
Orchard, The. Sto S —3C **50**
Orchard Way. Sys —6G **7**
Orchid Clo. Ham —3C **22**
Orchid Clo. Nar —2C **42**
Oriel Dri. Sys —6F **7**
Oriel Ho. Leic —1A **30**
Orkney Way. Count —2G **55**
Orlando Rd. Leic —5D **28**
Orme Clo. Leic —2E **19**
Ormen Grn. Leic —1B **26**
Oronsay Rd. Leic —2F **19**
Orpine Rd. Ham —2B **22**
Orson Dri. Wig —6D **36**
Orson St. Leic —2F **29**
Orton Rd. Leic —2A **20**
Orwell Dri. Leic —1E **19**
Osborne Rd. Leic —2F **29**
Osiers, The. Leic —2D **34**
Osmaston Rd. Leic —3E **29**
Osprey Clo. B Ast —6A **52**
Osprey Rd. Leic —5A **12**
Oswin Rd. Leic —2C **26**

Ottawa Rd. Leic —6C **20** (2F **4**)
Otter Way. Whet —6H **43**
Outfields Dri. Crop —1H **11**
Outwood Clo. Leic —2B **26**
Oval, The. Leic —3C **28** (7F **5**)
Oval, The. Oad —5H **37**
Oval, The. Sto S —3C **50**
Overdale Av. Glen —3H **17**
Overdale Clo. Glen —3H **17**
Overdale Rd. Leic —3D **36**
Overdale Rd. Thurm —5D **14**
Overfield Clo. Nar —4C **42**
Overfield Clo. Rat —5D **16**
Overfield Wlk. Rat —4D **16**
(in two parts)
Overing Clo. Leic —2C **20**
Overpark Av. Leic —3D **26**
Overseal Rd. Leic —5C **18**
Overton Rd. Leic —6F **21**
Owen Clo. Leic —6C **14**
Owston Dri. Wig —6D **36**
Oxendon St. Leic —2D **28**
Oxendon Wlk. Leic —2D **28**
Oxford Av. Leic —4D **28**
Oxford Ct. Sys —5G **7**
Oxford Dri. Wig —1F **45**
Oxford Rd. Leic —5D **28**
Oxford St. Leic —2A **28** (5B **5**)
Oxford St. Sys —5G **7**
Oxon Way. Leic —1A **30**
Oxted Rise. Oad —6A **38**

Packer Av. Leic F —3H **25**
Packhorse Grn. Leic —6H **35**
Packhorse Rd. Leic —6H **35**
Packman Grn. Count —2F **55**
Packwood Rd. Leic —2A **20**
Paddock Clo. Count —1E **55**
Paddock Clo. Oad —3H **37**
Paddocks, The. L'thrpe —4F **43**
Paddock St. Wig —1B **46**
Paddock, The. Kib —5A **62**
Paddock, The. Mark —2C **8**
Paddock View. Sys —6D **6**
Padgate Clo. Scrap —6F **23**
Padstow Rd. Leic —2G **21**
Padwell La. Bush —3F **31**
Paget Av. Bir —4H **13**
Paget Rd. Leic —1G **27**
Paget St. Kib —5A **62**
Paget St. Leic —3G **35**
Paigle Rd. Leic —3G **35**
Painter St. Leic —5C **20**
Palfreyman La. Oad —5E **39**
Palmer M. Mark —3C **8**
Palmerston Boulevd. Leic
—3E **37**
Palmerstone Clo. Kib —5H **59**
Palmerston Way. Leic —3E **37**
Palmer St. Leic —2C **20**
Pamela Pl. Leic —1A **20**
Pankhurst Rd. Leic —5A **12**
Paper Mill Clo. Ans —5F **11**
Parade, The. Flec —6B **58**
Parade, The. Oad —3A **38**
Paramore Clo. Whet —6A **44**
Pares St. Leic —6B **20**
Park Av. Leic —1A **36**

Park Av. Mark —2B **8**
Park Clo. Cosb —3F **53**
Park Cres. Oad —5C **38**
Parkdale Rd. Thurm —5C **14**
Park Dri. Glen —5A **18**
Park Dri. Leic —4A **26**
Parker Dri. Leic —4H **19**
Parkfield Clo. Rat —5D **16**
Park Hill Av. Leic —2H **35**
Park Hill Dri. Leic —2H **35**
Park Ho. Clo. Bir —6G **13**
Parkland Dri. Oad —3A **38**
(in three parts)
Parklands Av. Grob —2D **16**
Park La. Leic —5F **29**
Park Rise. Leic —2C **26**
Park Rd. Ans —6F **11**
Park Rd. Bir —5F **13**
Park Rd. Blab —3A **44**
Park Rd. Cosb —3F **53**
Park Rd. Nar —4D **42**
Park Rd. Rat —6D **16**
Park Rd. Sap —6B **50**
Park Rd. Wig —3F **45**
Parkside. Grob —1F **17**
Parkside Clo. Leic —5A **12**
Parkstone Clo. Wig —3A **46**
Parkstone Rd. Leic —5D **22**
Parkstone Rd. Sys —4F **7**
Park St. Flec —5B **58**
Park St. Leic —2B **28** (5D **5**)
Park Vale Rd. Leic —2E **29**
Park View. Leic —1C **26**
Parkway, The. Leic —6B **22**
Parlour Clo. Wig —1A **46**
Parry St. Leic —6E **21**
Parsons Dri. Glen P —6E **35**
Partridge Clo. Sys —5D **6**
Partridge Rd. Thurm —6D **14**
Parvian Rd. Leic —5C **36**
Pasley Clo. Leic —5H **35**
Pasley Rd. Leic —5H **35**
Pasture La. Leic
—6A **20** (1B **4**)
Pastures, The. B Ast —2B **60**
Pastures, The. Nar —3C **42**
Pastures, The. Sys —6C **6**
Paterson Clo. Leic —5A **12**
Paton St. Leic —3H **27**
Patterdale Rd. Thurm —5C **14**
Paul Dri. Leic —1H **21**
Pauline Av. Leic —1D **20**
Pawley Clo. Whet —5A **44**
Pawley Gdns. Leic —5H **35**
Pawley Grn. Leic —5H **35**
Payne St. Leic —2D **20**
Peacock Dri. Whet —6H **43**
Peacock La. Leic
—2A **28** (4B **4**)
Peakdale. Wig —2D **46**
Peake Rd. Leic —4F **21**
Peartree Clo. Ans —6F **11**
Peartree Clo. Glen —6H **17**
Peatling La. Count —2F **55**
Pedlars Clo. Leic —2F **19**
Pedlars Way. E Gos —2H **7**
Peebles Way. Leic —2F **21**
Peel Clo. Kib —5H **59**
Peewit Clo. Glen P —6E **35**

Pegasus Clo. Leic —2D **28**
Peldon Clo. Leic —3H **19**
Pelham St. Leic —3B **28** (6C **5**)
Pelham St. Oad —3A **38**
Pelham Way. Leic
—3B **28** (6C **5**)
Pells Clo. Flec —5B **58**
Pembroke Av. Sys —1F **15**
Pembroke Av. Wig —1F **45**
Pembroke St. Leic —6E **21**
Pembury Clo. Gt G —2D **48**
Pen Clo. Leic —5A **36**
Penclose Rd. Flec —5A **58**
Pendene Rd. Leic —6E **29**
Pendlebury Dri. Leic —2C **36**
Pendragon Way. Leic F —5G **25**
Penfold Clo. Sap —5B **50**
Penfold Dri. Count —2D **54**
Penhale Rd. Leic —1D **34**
Penkridge Wlk. Leic —1A **20**
Pennant Clo. Glen —6B **18**
Penney Clo. Wig —6E **37**
Pennine Way. Oad —4D **38**
Penny Long La. Leic F —4F **25**
Penrith Rd. Leic —3E **21**
Penryn Dri. Wig —2A **46**
Pensilva Clo. Wig —2A **46**
Pentridge Clo. Wig —3A **46**
Penzance Av. Wig —2A **46**
Peppercorn Clo. Leic —2G **19**
Peppercorn Wlk. Leic —2H **19**
Percival St. Leic —6F **21**
Percy Rd. Leic —2A **36**
Percy St. Leic —1E **35**
Peregrine Rise. Leic —5A **12**
Peregrine Rd. B Ast —5A **52**
Perkyn Rd. Leic —1C **30**
Perseverance Rd. Bir —6G **13**
Perth Av. Leic —6E **19**
(in two parts)
Peter's Clo. Sto S —3A **50**
Peters Dri. Leic —6B **22**
Petersfield. Cft —1G **51**
Petunia Clo. Leic F —5F **25**
Petworth Dri. Leic —1F **27**
Pevensey Av. Leic —4D **30**
Peverel Ct. Leic —6C **26**
Peverel Rd. Leic —5E **27**
Peveril Rd. Ash M —5H **61**
Philips Cres. Leic —5B **12**
Phillip Dri. Glen P —2E **45**
Phipps Clo. Whet —5A **44**
Phoenix Clo. Leic —6F **19**
Piccaver Rise. Leic —2B **26**
Pickering Clo. Leic —4F **21**
Pickering Rd. B Ast —3B **60**
Pickwell Clo. Leic —5C **18**
Piers Rd. Glen —4A **18**
Pilgrim Gdns. Leic —4A **30**
Pilkington Rd. Leic —4C **26**
Pimpernel Clo. Nar —2B **42**
Pindar Rd. Leic —5E **19**
Pine Dri. Sys —1F **15**
Pine Rd. Glen —5A **18**
Pinc Tree Av. Grob —3F **17**
Pine Tree La. Leic —6A **22**
Pine Tree Clo. Oad —5B **38**
Pine Tree Garden. Oad —5B **38**
Pine Tree Gro. Leic F —5E **25**

Pine Tree Wlk. Leic —5A **22**
Pinewood Av. Thurm —6C **14**
Pinewood Clo. Count —1E **55**
Pinewood Clo. Leic —6A **12**
Pinfold. Leic —2D **34**
Pinfold Rd. Thurm —5B **14**
Pingle La. Cft —5C **40**
Pingle St. Leic —6A **20** (1A **4**)
Pintail Clo. Whet —1H **53**
Piper Clo. Leic —6E **19**
Piper Way. Leic —6E **19**
Pipewell Wlk. Leic —2A **20**
Pitchens Clo. Leic —6H **11**
Pitton Clo. Wig —3A **46**
Pitts Av. Leic —2C **34**
Plantation Av. Leic —3G **35**
Plantation, The. Count —1E **55**
Platts La. Costn —2A **6**
Player Clo. Leic —6B **14**
Pleasant Clo. Leic F —5F **25**
Plough Clo. Leic F —6F **25**
Ploughmans' Lea. E Gos —2H **7**
Plover Cres. Leic —5B **12**
Plowman Clo. Glen —4A **18**
Plumtree Way. Sys —1F **15**
Pluto Clo. Leic —2D **28**
Plymouth Dri. Leic —4H **29**
Plymstock Clo. Leic —1F **27**
Poachers Clo. Glen —5H **17**
Poachers Pl. Oad —5D **38**
Pochin's Bri. Rd. Wig —3G **45**
Pochins Clo. Wig —2A **46**
Pochin St. Cft —1G **51**
Pockingtons Wlk. Leic
—2B **28** (5C **5**)
Polaris Clo. Leic —2D **28**
Pollard Rd. Leic —4C **26**
Pomeroy Dri. Oad —4H **37**
Pool Rd. Leic —1F **27**
Pope Cres. End —6G **33**
Pope St. Leic —1C **36**
Poplar Av. Bir —3G **13**
Poplar Av. Count —2E **55**
Poplar Av. Mark —3B **8**
Poplar Rd. L'thrpe —5D **42**
Poplars Clo. Grob —2E **17**
Poplars Farm Ct. Count —1F **55**
Poplars, The. Braun —2E **35**
Poplars, The. Rat —4B **16**
Poplar Ter. Ans —5F **11**
Poppins, The. Leic —5B **12**
Popple Clo. B Ast —2C **60**
Poppy Clo. Leic —5B **36**
Porlock St. Leic —2F **27**
Portcullis Rd. Leic —4E **23**
Portgate. Wig —2C **46**
Portishead Rd. Leic —5G **21**
Portland Building. Leic —6B **5**
Portland Gdns. Cosb —1F **53**
Portland Rd. Kir M —3E **25**
Portland Rd. Leic —6E **29**
Portland St. Cosb —1F **53**
Portland Towers. Leic —1G **37**
Portland Wlk. Oad —6C **38**
Portloc Dri. Wlg —3B **46**
Portman St. Leic —3D **20**
Portmore Clo. Leic —3G **19**
Portsdown Rd. Leic —3F **37**
Portslade Ho. Leic —1B **26**

80 A-Z Leicester

Portsmouth Rd. Leic —4C **20**
Portwey, The. Leic —5G **21**
Post Office La. New H —5H **47**
Post Rd. Thurm —2C **14**
Potters Marston La. Thurl
—3C **40**
Potter St. Leic —1C **28** (2E **4**)
Potterton Rd. Leic —1H **19**
Pougher Clo. Sap —6C **50**
Powys Av. Leic —6G **29**
Powys Gdns. Leic —6G **29**
Poynings Av. Leic —1E **27**
Probond St. Leic
—3C **28** (6F **5**)
Preston Rise. Leic —4C **22**
Prestwold Rd. Leic —5E **21**
Pretoria Rd. Kir M —2D **24**
Price Way. Thurm —4D **14**
Priestley Rd. Leic —2E **27**
Priest Meadow. Flec —5B **58**
Primethorpe Wlk. B Ast —6A **52**
Primrose Clo. Nar —3C **42**
Primrose Hill. Oad —3H **37**
Primrose Way. Kir M —1F **25**
Primrose Way. Quen —3H **7**
Prince Albert Dri. Glen —6A **18**
Prince Dri. Oad —4C **38**
Princes Clo. Ans —5G **11**
Princess Av. Oad —5C **38**
Princess Dri. Kir M   3D **24**
Princess Rd. Backways. Leic
—3B **28** (6D **5**)
Princess Rd. E. Leic
—3C **28** (7E **5**)
Princess Rd. Halls. Leic —6E **5**
Princess Rd. W. Leic
—3B **28** (6D **5**)
Princess St. Nar —3E **43**
Priory Clo. Sys —6D **6**
Priory Cres. Leic —2C **26**
Priory Wlk. Leic F —4G **25**
Progress Way. Leic —2A **22**
Prospect Hill. Leic —1E **29**
Prospect Rd. Kib —5H **59**
Prospect Rd. Leic —1F **29**
Pulford Dri. Thurn —1F **31**
(in two parts)
Pullman Rd. Wig —6D **36**
Purbeck Clo. Wig —3B **46**
Purcell Rd. Leic —5C **20**
Purley Rd. Leic —4E **21**
Putney Rd. Leic —5B **28**
Putney Rd. W. Leic —5B **28**
Pymm Leys Clo. Grob —2F **17**
Pymm Leys Gdns. Grob
—2F **17**
Pymm Leys La. Grob —3F **17**
Pytchley Clo. Leic —6E **13**

Quadrant, The. Leic —3B **20**
Quarry La. End —5G **33**
Quebec Rd. Leic —1C **28** (2F **4**)
Queens Dri. Leic F —4G **25**
Queens Dri. Nar —1F **43**
Queens Dri. Wig —1H **45**
Queensferry Pde. Leic —6G **35**
Queensgate Dri. Bir —3E **13**
Queensmead Clo. Grob —3E **17**

Queens Pk. Way. Leic —1D **44**
(in two parts)
Queen's Rd. Blab —4A **44**
Queens Rd. Leic —5D **28**
Queen St. Bark —5G **15**
Queen St. Leic —2C **28** (3E **4**)
Queen St. Mark —3B **8**
Queen St. Oad —3B **38**
Quemby Clo. Leic —3C **20**
Quenby Cres. Sys —6G **7**
Quenby St. Leic —6F **21**
Queniborough Ind. Est. Quen
—4H **7**
Queniborough Rd. Bark
—3H **15**
Queniborough Rd. Leic —4E **21**
Quiney Way. Oad —3C **38**
Quinton Rise. Oad —5A **38**
Quorn Av. Oad —5D **38**
Quorndon Rise. Grob —3E **17**
Quorn Rd. Leic —6F **21**

Radcot Lawns. Leic —6H **35**
Radford Dri. Leic —4A **26**
Radiant Rd. Leic —6C **22**
Radnor Ct. Nar —1B **42**
Radnor Rd. Wig —6C **36**
Radstone Wlk. Leic —1H **29**
Raeburn Rd. Leic —6D **28**
Ragdale Rd. Leic —4F **21**
Railway St. Wig —3F **45**
Raine Way. Oad —6D **38**
Rainsford Cres. Leic —2A **20**
Ralphs Clo. Dun B —5F **61**
Ramsbury Rd. Leic —4C **36**
Ramsdean Av. Wig —6E **37**
Ramsey Gdns. Leic —4E **23**
Ramsey Way. Leic —4E **23**
Rancliffe Cres. Leic —3E **27**
Randles Clo. Bush —3F **31**
Rannock Clo. Leic —2G **19**
Ranton Way. Leic —5G **19**
Ranworth Wlk. Leic —1A **20**
Ratby La. Kir M & Leic F
—6E **17**
Ratby La. Mark —4C **8**
Ratby Meadow La. Nar —6C **34**
Ratby Rd. Grob —3D **16**
Ratcliffe. Leic —1E **37**
Ratcliffe Ct. Leic —1F **37**
Ratcliffe Dri. Hunc —4H **41**
Ratcliffe Rd. Leic —1E **37**
Ratcliffe St. Leic —3D **20**
Ravenbridge Dri. Leic —5H **19**
Ravenhurst Rd. Leic —6D **26**
Raven Rd. Leic —4C **26**
Ravensthorpe Rd. Wig —1C **46**
Raw Dykes Rd. Leic —5A **28**
Rawlings Ct. Oad —5E **39**
Rawlings Pas. Oad —3A **38**
Rawlinson Wlk. Leic —2G **19**
Rawson St. End —6H **33**
Rawson St. Leic
—3C **28** (6D **5**)
Rawsthorne Wlk. Leic —5C **20**
Rayleigh Grn. Leic —4E **23**
Rayleigh Way. Leic —4E **23**
Raymond Rd. Leic —4G **27**

Rayner Rd. Leic —1G **21**
Rearsby Rd. Leic —4E **21**
Rectory Clo. Wig —2A **46**
Rectory Gdns. Leic —5B **30**
Rectory La. Kib —4A **62**
Rectory La. Thurc —1B **12**
Rectory Rd. Mark —2C **8**
Rectory Rd. Wan & Birs —6A **6**
Redcar Rd. Leic —4D **20**
Red Hill. Bir —6G **13**
Red Hill Av. Nar —3C **42**
Red Hill Circ. Leic —1B **20**
Red Hill Clo. Thurm —3C **14**
Red Hill La. Thurm —3C **14**
Red Hill Way. Leic —6C **12**
Red Ho. Clo. Leic —6G **35**
Red Ho. Gdns. Leic —5G **35**
Red Ho. Rise. Leic —5G **35**
Red Ho. Rd. Leic —5G **35**
Redmarle Rd. Leic —4E **27**
Redpath Clo. Leic —6D **20**
Redruth Av. Wig —2A **46**
Redwing Ct. Leic —6E **21**
Redwood Wlk. Leic —6E **21**
Reed Pool Clo. Count —1F **55**
Rees Gro. Leic —6B **14**
Reeth Clo. Leic —2G **19**
Reeves Clo. Whet —6H **43**
Regency Clo. Glen P —2D **44**
Regent Clo. Wig —1H **45**
Regent Rd. Count —1F **55**
Regent Rd. Leic
—3B **28** (6D **5**)
Regent St. Leic —3C **28** (6F **5**)
Regent St. Nar —3E **43**
Regent St. Oad —3A **38**
Regents Wlk. Leic F —4G **25**
Rendell Rd. Leic —4C **20**
Renfrew Rd. Leic —5E **23**
Renishaw Dri. Leic —5G **29**
Repington Row. Leic —4B **36**
Repton Rd. Wig —5D **36**
Repton St. Leic —6H **19**
Reservoir Rd. Crop —1G **11**
Retreat, The. Leic —2H **29**
Reynolds Pl. Leic —5E **27**
Ribble Av. Oad —3D **38**
Richard Clo. Leic —4A **26**
Richardson Clo. Sto S —4B **50**
Richardsons Clo. B Ast —2C **60**
Richard III Rd. Leic
—1H **27** (3A **4**)
Richmond Av. Leic —1A **36**
Richmond Clo. Cosb —3E **53**
Richmond Clo. Leic —1A **36**
Richmond Dri. Glen P —2E **45**
Richmond Rd. Leic —1A **36**
Richmond St. Leic
—3A **28** (6B **5**)
Richmond Way. Oad —6C **38**
Riddington Rd. Leic —2D **34**
Riddington Rd. L'thrpe —5E **43**
Ridgemere Clo. Sys —5H **7**
Ridgemere La. Quen —6H **7**
Ridgeway. L'thrpe —5E **43**
Ridgeway. Oad —6B **38**
Ridgeway Dri. Thurm —5D **14**
Ridgeway, The. Leic —6E **19**
Ridgway Rd. Leic —1F **37**

Ridings, The. Quen —4H **7**
Riding, The. Leic —5B **12**
Ridley Clo. Blab —5A **44**
Ridley Clo. Crop —1H **11**
Ridley St. Leic —3H **27**
Riley Clo. Sto S —4B **50**
Ringers Clo. Leic —1A **38**
Ringers Spinney. Oad —1A **38**
Ring Rd. Leic —3F **37**
(in three parts)
Ringwood Clo. Wig —2A **46**
Ringwood Rd. Leic —4E **23**
Ripon Dri. Blab —5B **44**
Ripon St. Leic —4E **29**
Rise, The. Nar —1C **42**
Riston Clo. Oad —6B **38**
Riversdale Clo. Bir —5H **13**
Riverside Clo. Gt G —2D **48**
Riverside Dri. Leic —3G **35**
Riverside Way. L'thrpe —4E **43**
Rivers St. Leic —1H **27**
Rivet's Meadow Clo. Leic
—6B **26**
Robert Hall St. Leic —2B **20**
Robertsbridge Av. Leic —2A **20**
Robertsbridge Wlk. Leic
—2A **20**
Robertson Clo. Sto S —3A **50**
Roberts Rd. Leic —4C **20**
Robin Clo. Leic —2A **36**
Robins Field. Rat —5D **16**
Robinson Rd. Leic —6H **21**
Robinson Way. Mark —3C **8**
Roborough Grn. Leic —1E **31**
Robotham Clo. Hunc —4A **42**
Roche Clo. Leic —5G **35**
Rochester Clo. Kib —3H **59**
Rockbridge Rd. Oad —5D **38**
Rockingham Clo. Blab —5B **44**
Rockingham Clo. Leic —1B **30**
Rockley Rd. Leic —4G **19**
Roebuck Clo. Leic —6H **43**
Roecliffe Clo. Mark —3C **8**
Roehampton Dri. Wig —4D **36**
Rogerstone Rd. Leic —3D **36**
Rolleston Rd. Wig —6D **36**
Rolleston Sq. Leic —1F **29**
Rolleston St. Leic —1F **29**
Roman Hill. Wig —3C **46**
Roman Rd. Bir —6G **13**
Roman St. Leic —3H **27**
Roman Way. Sys —1C **14**
Romway Av. Leic —5G **29**
Romway Rd. Leic —5G **29**
Rona Gdns. Leic —6E **23**
Ronald Ct. Leic —6E **29**
Rookery Clo. Kib —5A **62**
Rookery La. Grob —2E **17**
Rookery La. Thurm —5B **54**
Rookery, The. Grob —2F **17**
Rosamund Av. Leic —1E **35**
Rose Acre Clo. Scrap —6F **23**
Rosebank Rd. Count —2F **55**
Rosebarn Way. Leic —4D **22**
Rosebery Av. Kib —5H **59**
Rosebery Rd. Ans —5G **11**
Rosebery St. Leic —1F **29**
Rose Cres. Leic F —5F **25**
Rosedale Av. Leic —3F **21**

Rosedale Rd. Wig —1D **46**
Rosedene Av. Thurm —5C **14**
Rose Farm Clo. Leic —3D **26**
Rosemead Dri. Oad —4A **38**
Rosendene Clo. Kir M —3F **25**
Roseneath Av. Leic —3G **21**
Rose St. Leic —3B **20**
Rose Tree Av. Bir —3G **13**
Roseway. Leic —2F **21**
Roslyn St. Leic —3E **29**
Rossett Dri. Leic —3H **19**
Rossetti Rd. End —6G **33**
Rosshill Cres. Leic —6E **23**
Ross's La. Wig —1B **46**
Ross Wlk. Leic —5C **20**
(in three parts)
Rotherby Av. Leic —4F **21**
Rothley St. Leic —5C **20**
Roughton St. Leic —3C **20**
Roundhay Rd. Leic —5G **27**
Roundhill. Kir M —2E **25**
Roundhill Clo. Sys —1D **14**
Roundhill Rd. Leic —4F **29**
Roundway, The. Leic —6D **14**
Rowanberry Av. Leic —1A **26**
Rowans, The. Count —1E **55**
Rowan St. Leic —1G **27**
Rowlandson Clo. Leic —2C **12**
Rowlands Way. Glen P —1B **44**
Rowlatts Hill Rd. Leic —1H **29**
Rowley Clo. Flec —6C **58**
Rowley Fields Av. Leic —6F **27**
Rowsley Av. Leic —3F **29**
Rowsley St. Leic —3E **29**
Royal Arc. Leic —3C **4**
Royal Ct. Nar —3E **43**
Royal E. St. Leic
—6B **20** (1D **4**)
Royal Kent St. Leic
—6A **20** (1B **4**)
Royal Rd. Leic —3D **20**
Roy Clo. Nar —3E **43**
Roydene Cres. Leic —3G **19**
Royston Clo. Leic —1C **44**
Ruby St. Leic —1G **27**
Ruddington Wlk. Leic —1A **20**
Ruding Rd. Leic —3H **27**
Ruding St. Leic —1A **28** (3A **4**)
(in two parts)
Ruding Ter. Leic —3H 27
(off Ruding Rd.)
Rufford St. Leic —1G **29**
Rugby St. Leic —6H **19**
Rumsey Dri. Whet —3A **44**
Runcorn Clo. Leic —6G **35**
Runcorn Rd. Leic —6G **35**
Runnymede Gdns. Glen —6B **18**
Rupert St. Leic —2B **28** (5C **5**)
Rupert's Way. Gt G —3D **48**
Rushden Ho. Leic —1A **26**
Rushes, The. Mark —2C **8**
Rushey Clo. Leic —1E **21**
Rushford Clo. Leic —4F **21**
Rushford Dri. Leic —4F **21**
Rushmere Wlk. Leic F —5G **25**
Rushton Dri. Leic —5F **35**
Ruskin Av. Sys —1G **15**
Ruskington Dri. Wig —4F **37**
Russell Ct. Leic —3G **35**

Russell Sq. Leic —6C **20**
Russet Way. Thurm —2A **14**
Rutherford Rd. Leic —1E **19**
Rutland Av. Leic —1A **36**
Rutland Av. Wig —6D **36**
Rutland Clo. Leic F —4G **25**
Rutland Dri. Thurm —4C **14**
Rutland St. Leic —2B **28** (4D **4**)
(in two parts)
Rydal Ho. Leic —6G **35**
Rydal St. Leic —3A **28** (7A **5**)
Ryde Av. Leic —2F **37**
Ryder Rd. Leic —1A **26**
Rye Clo. Leic —5A **36**
Ryegate Cres. Bir —3F **13**

Sacheverell Way. Grob
—4D **16**
Sacheverel Rd. Leic —1B **26**
Sackville Gdns. Leic —1E **37**
Saddington Rd. Flec —6B **58**
Saddlers' Clo. E Gos —2H **7**
Saddlers Clo. Glen —5H **17**
Saffron Hill Rd. Leic —1A **36**
Saffron La. Leic & Wig —5A **28**
Saffron Rd. Wig —6A **36**
Saffron Way. Leic —3A **36**
Sahara Clo. Leic —2D **20**
St Aidan's Av. Sys —6D **6**
St Albans Rd. Leic —3D **28**
St Andrews Dri. Leic —6G **29**
St Andrew's Rd. Leic —2A **36**
St Annes Clo. Sys —1G **15**
St Anne's Dri. Leic —3H **35**
St Augustine Rd. Leic
—2H **27** (4A **4**)
St Austell Rd. Leic —6E **23**
St Barnabas Rd. Leic —1G **29**
St Bernard's Av. Leic —2D **20**
St Bernard St. Leic —2D **20**
Saintbury Rd. Glen —4B **18**
St Columba Way. Sys —5D **6**
St Crispins Way. Thurm
—2C **14**
St Cuthbert's Av. Gt G —3D **48**
St Davids Clo. Leic F —4F **25**
St David's Cres. Leic —6G **29**
St Denys Rd. Leic —3B **30**
St Dunstan Rd. Leic —1G **27**
St George's Retail Pk. Leic
—1D **28**
St George's St. Leic
—2C **28** (4F **4**)
St George's Way. Leic
—2C **28** (4F **4**)
St Helens Clo. Leic —4G **19**
St Helens Dri. Leic —4H **19**
St Hilda's Clo. Sys —1G **15**
St Ives Rd. Leic —3G **21**
St Ives Rd. Wig —2A **46**
St James Clo. Hunc —4H **41**
St James Clo. Oad —6C **38**
St James Ct. Bir —5H **13**
St James Rd. Leic —4E **29**
St James St. Leic
—1C **28** (3E **4**)
St James Ter. Leic —4E **29**
St John's Av. Sys —1G **15**

St Johns Rd. Leic —5E **29**
St John St. Leic —6B **20** (1C **4**)
St Johns Wlk. Leic —5E **5**
St Leonard's Ct. Leic —5D **28**
St Leonard's Rd. Leic —5D **28**
St Luke's Clo. Thurn —3F **31**
St Margaret's St. Leic
—6A **20** (1C **4**)
St Margaret's Way. Leic
—5A **20** (1B **4**)
St Margarets Way. Leir —6A **60**
St Mark's St. Leic —6C **20**
St Martins. Leic —2B **28** (4C **4**)
St Martins E. Leic
—2B **28** (4C **4**)
St Martins Sq. Shopping Cen.
Leic —2B **28** (4C **4**)
St Martins Wlk. Leic
—2A **28** (4B **4**)
St Mary's Av. Braun —4A **26**
St Mary's Av. Hum —5C **22**
St Mary's Clo. B Ast —1A **60**
St Marys Ct. Braun —4A **26**
St Mary's Ct. Hum —5C **22**
St Mary's Rd. Leic —5D **28**
St Matthew's Way. Leic
—6C **20** (1E **4**)
St Maxine Ct. Leic —6E **29**
St Mellion Clo. Leic —4B **12**
St Michael's Av. Leic —2D **20**
St Michael's Clo. Mark —2B **8**
St Michael's Ct. Sto S —3B **50**
St Michael's Ct. Thurm —4C **14**
St Nicholas Circ. Leic
—2A **28** (4A **4**)
St Nicholas Pl. Leic
—2A **28** (4B **4**)
St Nicholas Wlk. Leic —2A 28
(off St Nicholas Circ.)
St Oswalds Rd. Leic —6D **18**
St Pauls Clo. Oad —3D **38**
St Pauls Ct. Sys —5E **7**
St Paul's Dri. Sys —1E **15**
St Pauls Rd. Leic —1G **27**
St Peter's Clo. Glen —5H **17**
St Peter's Clo. Leir —6B **60**
St Peter's Ct. Sys —5F **7**
St Peter's Dri. Whet —3H **43**
St Peter's La. Leic
—1A **28** (3B **4**)
St Peters Path. Leic —4A **38**
St Peter's Rd. Leic —3D **28**
St Peter's St. Sys —6E **7**
St Phillip's Rd. Leic —4F **29**
St Saviour's Hill. Leic —1E **29**
St Saviour's Rd. Leic —1E **29**
St Saviour's Wlk. Leic —2H **29**
St Stephens Rd. Leic —3E **29**
St Swithin's Rd. Leic —2D **30**
St Thomas Rd. Wig —2E **45**
St Thomas's Rd. Gt G —2E **49**
St Wilfrid's Clo. Kib —4A **62**
St Wolstan's Clo. Wig —6F **37**
Salcombe Clo. Wig —2A **46**
Salcombe Dri. Glen —5A **18**
Salisbury Av. Cft —1G **51**
Salisbury Av. Leic —3D **28**
Salisbury Clo. Blab —5B **44**
Salisbury Rd. Leic —4D **28**

Salkeld Rd. Leic —1C **44**
Saltash Clo. Wig —2A **46**
Saltcoats Av. Leic —1E **21**
Saltersford Rd. Leic —6H **21**
Saltersgate Dri. Bir —3G **13**
Salts Clo. End —1D **42**
Samson Rd. Leic —6F **19**
Samuel St. Leic —1C **28**
Sandacre St. Leic
—1B **28** (2C **4**)
Sanderson Clo. Whet —5A **44**
Sanderson Wlk. Sys —5F **7**
Sandfield Clo. Leic —6C **14**
Sandford Clo. Leic —1A **30**
Sandford Ct. Leic —1A **30**
Sandford Rd. Sys —6E **7**
Sandgate Av. Bir —3F **13**
Sandhill Dri. Nar —1F **43**
Sandhills Av. Leic —2A **22**
Sandhurst Clo. Leic —1F **27**
Sandhurst Rd. Leic —6F **19**
Sandhurst St. Oad —3A **38**
Sandiacre Dri. Thurm —3D **14**
Sandown Rd. Glen —4A **18**
Sandown Rd. Leic —6F **29**
Sandown Rd. Wig —5F **37**
Sandpiper Clo. Leic —6E **21**
Sandringham Av. Leic —2D **20**
Sandringham Rd. Glen P
—2E **45**
Sandy Rise. Wig —5H **37**
Sanvey Clo. Leic —3G **35**
Sanvey Ga. Leic —1A **28** (2A **4**)
Sanvey La. Leic —3F **35**
Sapcote Rd. Sto S —3C **50**
Saunderson Rd. Leic —1H **19**
Savernake Rd. Leic —4G **19**
Saville Rd. Blab —5C **44**
Saville St. Leic —1G **29**
Sawbrook. Flec —6C **58**
Sawday St. Leic —4A **28**
Sawley Dri. Leic —4F **29**
Saxby St. Leic —3D **28**
Saxondale Rd. Wig —3C **46**
Saxons Rise. Rat —4C **16**
Saxon St. Leic —3H **27**
Scalborough Clo. Count
—1C **54**
Scalpay Clo. Leic —2F **19**
Scarborough Rd. Leic —3E **21**
Scarptoft Rise. Scrap —5F **23**
Schaeffer Ct. Leic —3F **19**
School Clo. Cft —2G **51**
School Cres. B Ast —6A **52**
Schoolgate. Leic —4B **36**
School Ho. Clo. Ans —6F **11**
School La. Bark —3H **15**
School La. Bir —5G **13**
School La. Evi —5B **30**
School La. Hunc —4H **41**
School La. Nar —4E **43**
School Rd. Kib —5A **62**
School St. Flec —6B **58**
School St. Sys —5F **7**
School Wlk. Kib —5A **62**
Scotland La. Bur O —2H **49**
Scotland Way. Count —2F **55**
Scotswood Cres. Leic —6G **35**
Scott St. Leic —1C **36**

Scraptoft La. Leic —6A **22**
Scraptoft La. Scrap —2H **23**
Scraptoft M. Leic —6A **22**
Scudamore Rd. Leic —2H **25**
Seaford Rd. Leic —4H **35**
Seagrave Dri. Oad —3H **37**
Seaton Rise. Leic —4E **23**
Seaton Rd. Wig —2A **46**
Seddons Clo. Leic —1H **19**
Sedgebrook Clo. Leic —3E **31**
Sedgebrook Rd. Leic —3D **30**
Sedgefield Dri. Sys —6C **6**
Sedgefield Dri. Thurn —1F **31**
Segrave Rd. Leic —5F **27**
Seine La. End —5F **33**
Selbury Dri. Oad —4H **37**
Selby Av. Leic —4D **22**
Selkirk Rd. Leic —1F **21**
Sence Cres. Gt G —3C **48**
Severn Clo. Cosb —2F **53**
Severn Rd. Oad —4C **38**
Severn St. Leic —3D **28**
Sextant Rd. Leic —6C **22**
Seymour Rd. Leic —6D **28**
Seymour St. Leic —3A **28**
Seymour Way. Leic F —5F **25**
Shackerdale Rd. Wig —5D **36**
Shackleton St. Leic —6C **20**
Shadrack Clo. Sto S —4B **50**
Shady La. Leic —6B **30**
Shaftesbury Av. Leic —3C **20**
Shaftesbury Rd. Leic —3G **27**
Shakespeare Clo. Leic —6C **26**
Shakespeare Dri. Leic —6D **26**
Shakespeare St. Leic —1B **36**
Shanklin Av. Leic —2F **37**
Shanklin Dri. Leic —2F **37**
Shanklin Gdns. Leic —2F **37**
Shanklin Gdns. Leic F —5H **25**
Shanklin Wlk. Leic —3F **37**
Shanti Margh. Leic —3E **21**
Shardlow Rd. Wig —6E **37**
Sharmon Cres. Leic —1B **26**
Sharnford Rd. Sap —6C **50**
Sharpland. Leic —4G **35**
Sharpley Dri. Leic —5A **12**
Sharpley Hill. New L —1H **9**
Shaw Clo. Whet —5H **43**
Shaw Wood Clo. Grob —2E **17**
Shearer Clo. Leic —1G **21**
Sheene Rd. Leic —1E **19**
Sheepwash La. Ans —5G **11**
Sheffield St. Leic —4H **27**
Shelbourne St. Leic —1E **29**
Sheldon St. Leic —1D **28**
Shelduck Clo. Whet —1H **53**
Shelford Wlk. Leic —2A **20**
Shelley Rd. Nar —1C **42**
Shelley St. Leic —1C **36**
Shenley Rd. Wig —5G **37**
Shenton Clo. Thurm —5E **15**
Shenton Clo. Whet —4H **43**
Shenton Clo. Wig —6E **37**
Shepherds Clo. Leic F —4E **25**
Shepherd's Wlk. E Gos —2H **7**
Sherborne Av. Wig —3B **46**
Sherford Clo. Wig —1A **46**
Sheridan Clo. Nar —1C **42**

Sheridan St. Leic —1B **36**
Sheringham Rd. Leic —3H **19**
Sherloyd Clo. Leic —1H **21**
Sherrard Rd. Leic —1E **29**
Sherrard Way. Braun —6B **26**
Sherwood St. Leic —1G **29**
Shetland Rd. Leic —3E **21**
Shetland Way. Count —1F **55**
Shield Cres. Leic —1C **44**
Shipley Rd. Leic —3F **29**
Shipston Hill. Oad —5A **38**
Shipton Clo. Wig —1D **46**
Shire Clo. Leic —2C **26**
Shires Cen., The. Leic
—1B **28** (3C **4**)
Shires La. Leic —1A **28** (3B **4**)
Shirley Av. Leic —1F **37**
Shirley Dri. Sys —4F **7**
Shirley Rd. Leic —1F **37**
Shirley St. Leic —3C **20**
Shortridge La. End —6H **33**
Short St. Leic —1B **28** (2C **4**)
Shottens Clo. Leic —3F **19**
Shottery Av. Leic —6D **26**
Shoulbard. Flec —5A **58**
Shrewsbury Av. Leic —3C **36**
Shropshire Rd. Leic —2H **35**
Shuttleworth La. Cosb —4E **53**
Sibson Rd. Bir —4G **13**
Sibton La. Oad —5A **38**
Sickleholm Dri. Leic —5G **29**
Sidings, The. Leic —1B **20**
Sidmouth Av. Leic —4A **30**
Sidney Rd. Leic —2F **37**
Sidwell St. Leic —2G **29**
Silbury Rd. Leic —4G **19**
Silsden Rise. Leic —6H **35**
Silver Arc. Leic —3C **4**
Silverbirch Way. E Gos —1H **7**
Silverdale Dri. Thurm —5D **14**
Silverstone Dri. Leic —6B **14**
(in two parts)
Silver St. Leic —1B **28** (3C **4**)
Silverton Rd. Oad —3C **38**
Silver Wlk. Leic —3C 4
(off Silver St.)
Silverwood Clo. Leic —2C **30**
Simmins Clo. Leic —5H **35**
Simmins Cres. Leic —5H **35**
Simons Clo. Wig —3C **46**
Simpson Clo. Whet —5A **44**
Siskin Hill. Glen —5H **17**
Sitch Clo. B Ast —2C **60**
Sitwell Wlk. Leic —5H **29**
Six Acres. B Ast —1A **60**
Skampton Grn. Leic —2B **30**
Skampton Rd. Leic —2B **30**
Skelton Dri. Leic —3C **36**
Sketchley Clo. Leic —1D **30**
Skipworth St. Leic —3E **29**
Skye Way. Count —2F **55**
Slade Greens, The. Leic
—5G **35**
Slade Pl. Leic —5G **35**
Slate Brook Clo. Grob —2F **17**
Slate Clo. Glen —5H **17**
Slater St. Leic —6A **20**
Slate St. Leic —2C **28** (5F **5**)
Sloane Clo. End —6G **33**

Smedmore Rd. Leic —5F **21**
Smeeton Rd. Kib —6A **62**
Smith Av. Thurm —5D **14**
Smith Dorrien Rd. Leic —6G **21**
Smithland Clo. Mark —3C **8**
Smithy Farm Dri. Sto S
—3A **50**
Smore Slade Hills. Oad —5E **39**
Snowdens End. Wig —2C **46**
Snowdrop Clo. Nar —3B **42**
Snow Hill. Leic —4G **19**
Soar La. Leic —1A **28** (2A **4**)
Soar Rd. Thurm —2C **14**
Soar Valley Way. Leic —5D **34**
Somerby Dri. Oad —4C **38**
Somerby Rd. Thurn —1F **31**
Somerfield Wlk. Leic —3F **19**
Somerfield Way. Leic F —5F **25**
Somerscales Wlk. Leic —6D **20**
Somerset Av. Leic —3H **19**
Somerset Dri. Glen —6H **17**
Somers Rd. Leic —1C **30**
Somerville Rd. Leic —6F **27**
Sonning Way. Glen P —1C **44**
Sopers Rd. Cft —2G **51**
Sorrell Rd. Leic —3C **22**
Sorrel Way. Nar —2B **42**
S. Albion St. Leic —2C **28** (5E **5**)
Southampton St. Leic
—1C **28** (3E **4**)
South Av. Leic F —4H **25**
South Av. Wig —1A **46**
S. Church Ga. Leic
—6A **20** (1B **4**)
Southdown Dri. Thurm —5C **14**
Southdown Rd. Leic —1F **29**
South Dri. Leic —5A **22**
South Dri. Sto S —4C **50**
Southernhay Av. Leic —6E **29**
Southernhay Clo. Leic —6E **29**
Southernhay Rd. Leic —1E **37**
Southey Clo. End —1C **42**
Southey Clo. Leic —5D **20**
Southfield Av. Sys —6F **7**
Southfield Clo. Glen P —6E **35**
Southfield Clo. Scrap —6F **23**
Southfields Av. Oad —3H **37**
Southfields Dri. Leic —4B **36**
(in two parts)
Southgates. Leic
—2A **28** (4B **4**)
Southgates Underpass. Leic
—2A **28** (4B **4**)
S. Kingsmead Rd. Leic —3E **37**
S. Knighton Rd. Leic —2F **37**
Southland Rd. Leic —3F **37**
Southmeads Clo. Leic —2H **37**
Southmeads Rd. Leic —2H **37**
South St. Oad —3A **38**
Southview Ct. Leic F —4F **25**
Southview Dri. Leic —5H **29**
South Wlk. Rat —4C **16**
Southway. Blab —5B **44**
South Way. Kib —4B **62**
Spa Dri. Sap —5B **50**
Spa La. Wig —1B **46**
Spalding St. Leic —1G **29**
Sparkenhoe. Cft —2G **51**
Sparkenhoe St. Leic —2D **28**

Speedwell Clo. Nar —2B **42**
Speedwell Dri. Ham —2B **22**
(in two parts)
Speers Rd. Leic —5C **18**
Spencefield Dri. Leic —4B **30**
Spencefield La. Leic —4B **30**
Spencer Av. Thurm —4C **14**
Spencer St. Oad —3A **38**
Spence St. Leic —6F **21**
Spendlow Gdns. Leic —5A **36**
(in two parts)
Spendlow Grn. Leic —5A **36**
Spinney Av. Count —1F **55**
Spinney Clo. Glen P —6E **35**
Spinney Clo. Grob —3E **17**
Spinney Clo. Sys —6C **6**
Spinney Ct. Cft —1G **51**
Spinney Dri. Kib —4A **62**
Spinney Halt. Whet —4G **43**
Spinney Hill Rd. Leic —6E **21**
Spinney Rise. Bir —4F **13**
Spinney Side. Grob —3E **17**
Spinney, The. Thurn —3E **31**
Spinney View. Gt G —2E **49**
Sponne Rise. Leic —5A **36**
Sportsfield La. Hunc —3H **41**
Sports Rd. Glen —5A **18**
Springbrook Dri. Scrap —1F **31**
Spring Clo. Leic —1G **35**
Spring Clo. Rat —5D **16**
Springdale Rd. Thurm —5C **14**
Springfield Clo. B Ast —2B **60**
Springfield Clo. Glen —6H **17**
Springfield Clo. Kib —6B **62**
Springfield Cres. Kib —6B **62**
(in two parts)
Springfield La. Sm W —6A **62**
Springfield Rd. Leic —5E **29**
Spring Gdns. L'thrpe —5E **43**
Spring Gdns. Sap —5C **50**
Spring La. Wig —6F **37**
Springway Clo. Leic —2E **31**
Springwell Clo. Count —1E **55**
Springwell Dri. Count —1D **54**
Springwell La. Whet —6H **43**
Square, The. Count —2F **55**
Square, The. Glen —4H **17**
Square, The. L'thrpe —5E **43**
Square, The. New H —5E **47**
Square, The. Sap —6B **50**
Square, The. Thurn —3F **31**
Squires Ride. E Gos —1H **7**
Squirrel Clo. Nar —4C **42**
Squirrel's Corner. E Gos —1H **7**
Stable Clo. L'thrpe —4E **43**
Stackley Rd. Gt G —2D **48**
Stadium Pl. Leic —3A **20**
Stadium Rise. Leic —4H **19**
Stadon Rd. Ans —5F **11**
Stafford Dri. Wig —1F **45**
Stafford Leys. Leic F —4F **25**
Stafford St. Leic —2E **21**
Stainmore Av. Nar —1C **42**
Stamford Clo. Glen —5H **17**
Stamford Clo. Rat —4C **16**
Stamford Dri. Crop —1H **11**
Stamford Dri. Grob —3F **17**
Stamford Hall. Oad —1H **37**
Stamford Rd. Kir M —3E **25**

Stamford St. Glen —4H **17**
Stamford St. Leic
                —2B **28** (5D **5**)
Stamford St. Rat —4B **16**
Stanbrig. Wig —3C **46**
Stancliff Rd. Leic —6D **14**
Standale. Wig —1D **46**
Stanfell Rd. Leic —1C **36**
Stanhope Rd. Wig —2C **46**
Stanhope St. Leic —2F **29**
Stanier Rd. B Ast —1C **60**
Stanley Dri. Leic —5A **22**
Stanley Rd. Leic —4E **29**
Stanton La. Pot M —1D **50**
Stanton La. Sap —5A **50**
Stanton Rd. Sap —5B **50**
Stanton Row. Leic —3B **36**
Stanyon Clo. Count —1E **55**
Stapleford Rd. Leic —1H **19**
Staplehurst Av. Leic —1C **34**
Station Clo. Kir M —3E **25**
Station Dri. Kir M —3E **25**
Station Hollow. Kib —5A **62**
Station La. Leir —6A **60**
Station La. Scrap —6F **23**
Station Rd. Bir —6F **13**
Station Rd. B Ast —2C **60**
Station Rd. Count —2D **54**
Station Rd. Cft —1G **51**
Station Rd. Crop —1G **11**
Station Rd. Dun B —5G **61**
Station Rd. Glen —4H **17**
Station Rd. Kir M —2D **24**
Station Rd. L'thrpe —4E **43**
Station Rd. Rat —5C **16**
Station Rd. Sto S —2A **50**
Station Rd. Sys —6E **7**
Station Rd. Thurn —2F **31**
Station Rd. Wig —1H **45**
Station St. Kib —5A **62**
Station St. Leic —2C **28** (5F **5**)
Station St. Whet —3H **43**
Station St. Wig —1G **45**
Staveley Clo. Wig —2C **46**
Staveley Rd. Leic —4F **29**
Steadman Av. Cosb —2G **53**
Stebbings Rd. Leic —4H **35**
Steele Clo. Leic —2A **30**
Steeple Clo. Wig —5G **37**
Steins La. Leic —5B **22**
Stemborough La. Leir —6B **60**
Stenor Clo. Flec —5A **58**
Stenson Rd. Leic —4E **19**
Stephenson. B Ast —3C **60**
Stephenson Clo. Grob —2E **17**
Stephenson Ct. Glen —3A **18**
Stephenson Dri. Leic —6F **19**
Stephenson Way. Grob —2E **17**
Stevens Clo. Nar —2D **42**
Stevens Clo. Sto S —3C **50**
Stevenson Gdns. Cosb —1F **53**
Stevenstone Clo. Oad —4D **38**
Stewart Av. Nar —2C **42**
Steyning Cres. Glen —4B **18**
Stibbe Building. Leic —6B **5**
Stiles Clo. B Ast —2B **60**
Stiles, The. Sys —5F **7**
(in two parts)

Stirling Dri. Thurn —1F **31**
Stockland Rd. Leic —5A **36**
Stocks Rd. Scrap —5F **23**
Stockton Ho. Leic —1A **26**
Stockton Rd. Leic —4G **21**
Stockwell Rd. Leic —3E **37**
Stokesby Rise. Glen P —2C **44**
Stokes Dri. Leic —5F **19**
Stonebridge St. Leic —1F **29**
Stonechat Wlk. Leic —1E **29**
Stone Clo. Leic —5B **12**
Stonecroft. Count —2C **54**
Stonehaven Rd. Leic —1F **21**
Stonehill Av. Bir —2G **13**
Stonehill Clo. Gt G —2E **49**
Stonehill Dri. Gt G —2E **49**
Stonehurst Rd. Leic —1D **34**
Stoneleigh Mnr. Leic —5F **29**
Stoneleigh Way. Leic —5F **19**
Stonesby Av. Leic —4A **36**
Stoneycote Ct. Leic —5E **29**
Stoneygate Av. Leic —6E **29**
Stoneygate Rd. Leic —5E **29**
Stoney La. Mark —2A **8**
Stoneywell Rd. Leic —6H **11**
Stores La. Flec —6B **58**
Storey St. Leic —6H **19**
Stornaway Rd. Leic —6D **22**
Stoughton Av. Leic —6F **29**
Stoughton Clo. Oad —3B **38**
Stoughton Dri. Leic —5H **29**
Stoughton Dri. N. Leic —4F **29**
Stoughton Dri. S. Leic —6H **29**
Stoughton La. Leic —5B **30**
Stoughton Rd. Leic —6F **29**
Stoughton Rd. Oad —3A **38**
Stoughton Rd. Thurn —4E **31**
Stoughton St. Leic —2D **28**
Stoughton St. S. Leic —2D **28**
Stour Clo. Oad —3D **38**
Strasbourg Dri. Leic —2E **19**
Stratford Rd. Leic —6D **26**
Strathaven Rd. Leic —1F **21**
Strathmore Av. Leic —3F **21**
Strawberry Gdns. Leic —5G **33**
Streamside Clo. B Ast —2B **60**
Strensall Rd. Leic —6H **35**
Stretton Ct. Gt G —3D **48**
Stretton Rd. Gt G & Oad
                —3D **48**
Stretton Rd. Leic —2G **27**
Strollers Way. E Gos —2H **7**
Stroma Way. Count —2F **55**
Stroud Rd. Leic —6F **21**
Strudwick Way. Whet —2A **44**
Stuart Ct. Leic —6E **29**
Stuart Rd. Glen P —6G **35**
Stuart St. Kib —5A **62**
Stuart St. Leic —4H **27**
Stubbs Rd. Leic —5D **20**
Sturdee Clo. Leic —6H **35**
Sturdee Grn. Leic —5G **35**
Sturdee Rd. Leic —5G **35**
(in three parts)
Sturrock Rd. Thurn —1F **31**
Styon Rd. Leic —4C **18**
Sudeley Av. Leic —3A **20**
Suffolk Clo. Wig —6C **36**
Suffolk St. Leic —2G **29**

Sulgrave Rd. Leic —6F **21**
Summerlea Rd. Leic —1C **30**
Sunbury Grn. Leic —6E **23**
(in three parts)
Sunbury Rise. Count —1C **54**
Sundew Rd. Ham —3C **22**
Sunningdale Rd. Leic —3H **25**
Sunnycroft Rd. Leic —2E **27**
Sunnyfield Clo. Leic —2C **30**
Sunnyside. Oad —5C **38**
Sun Way. Leic —4B **26**
Surrey St. Leic —4D **20**
Susan Av. Leic —3B **30**
Sussex Rd. Wig —6B **36**
Sussex St. Leic —1D **28**
Sutherington Way. Ans —4G **11**
Sutherland St. Leic —3E **29**
Sutton Av. Leic —4E **21**
Sutton Clo. Oad —6B **38**
Sutton Pl. Leic —3E **21**
Sutton Rd. Leic —2C **36**
Swainson Rd. Leic —5G **21**
Swain St. Leic —2C **28** (4F **4**)
Swale Clo. Oad —3D **38**
Swallow Clo. Leic F —6E **25**
Swallowdale Dri. Leic —5B **12**
Swallow Dri. Sys —5C **6**
Swallows Dale. E Gos —1H **7**
Swannington Rd. B Ast —1C **60**
Swannington Rd. Leic —6G **19**
Swanscombe Rd. Leic —6H **27**
Swan St. Leic —1A **28** (2A **4**)
Swan Way. Sys —5C **6**
Sweetbriar Rd. Leic —4G **27**
Swift Clo. Sys —5D **6**
Swinford Av. Leic —1D **44**
Swinford Ct. Leic —1D **44**
Swinstead Rd. Leic —3D **30**
Swithland Av. Leic —4A **20**
Swithland Ct. Leic —2D **34**
Sword Clo. Glen —6A **18**
Sybil Rd. Leic —6F **27**
Sycamore Clo. Leic —6G **29**
Sycamore Clo. Sys —1F **15**
Sycamore Dri. Grob —3F **17**
Sycamore Gro. Grob —2F **17**
Sycamore Rd. Bir —2G **13**
Sycamore St. Blab —3B **44**
Sycamore Way. L'thrpe
                —5D **42**
Sykefield Av. Leic —3G **27**
Sylvan Av. Leic —1F **29**
Sylvan St. Leic —1G **27**
Sylvan Way. Leic F —3H **25**
Syston By-Pass. Sys —4C **6**
Syston Northern By-Pass. Sys
                —3E **7**
Syston Rd. Costn —2A **6**
Syston Rd. Quen —3H **7**
Syston St. E. Leic —6D **20**
Syston St. W. Leic —5C **20**
Sywell Dri. Wig —1C **46**

Tadcaster Av. Leic —6H **35**
Tadcaster Grn. Leic —6H **35**
Tailby Av. Leic —5G **21**
Tailors Link. E Gos —2H **7**
Talbot La. Leic —2A **28** (4A **4**)

Talbot St. Leic —2C **20**
Tall Trees. Sto S —2C **50**
Tamar Rd. Leic —3G **21**
Tamar Rd. Oad —3D **38**
Tamerton Rd. Leic —4A **36**
Tansey Cres. Sto S —3A **50**
Tansley Av. Wig —2G **45**
Tarbat Rd. Leic —6D **22**
Tatlow Ho. Leic —1A **26**
Tatlow Rd. Glen —1A **26**
Taunton Clo. Wig —2A **46**
Taunton Rd. Leic —2F **27**
Taurus Clo. Leic —2D **28**
Taverner Dri. Rat —6D **16**
Taverners Rd. Leic —4C **12**
Tavistock Dri. Leic —4H **29**
Taylor Clo. Sto S —3B **50**
Taylor Clo. Sys —6E **7**
Taylor Rd. Leic —6C **20**
Taylor's Bri. Rd. Wig —2G **45**
Teal Clo. Leic F —5E **25**
Teal Way. Sys —5C **6**
Teasel Clo. Nar —3C **42**
Tebbs Clo. Count —1C **54**
Tedworth Grn. Leic —6D **12**
(in two parts)
Teesdale Clo. Leic
                —4A **28** (7B **5**)
Teignmouth Clo. Leic —4H **29**
Teignmouth Wlk. Leic —4H **29**
Telford Way. Leic —2E **31**
Tempest Rd. Bir —6F **13**
Temple Rd. Leic —2G **29**
Tendring Dri. Wig —6H **37**
Tennis Ct. Dri. Leic —6A **22**
Tennyson St. Leic —4E **29**
Tennyson St. Nar —2C **42**
Tentercroft Av. Sys —5G **7**
Terrace Cotts. Cft —1G **51**
Tetuan Rd. Leic —1F **27**
Tewkesbury St. Leic —1H **27**
Thackeray St. Leic —1B **36**
Thames St. Leic —6B **20** (1D **4**)
Thatcher Clo. Leic —1F **19**
Thatchers Corner. E Gos —2H **7**
Thirlmere Rd. Wig —6G **37**
Thirlmere St. Leic —4A **28**
Thistle Clo. Crop —1H **11**
Thistle Clo. Nar —3C **42**
Thomasson Rd. Leic —1B **30**
Thomson Clo. Leic —5B **14**
Thoresby St. Leic —1G **29**
Thornborough Clo. Nar —4B **42**
Thornby Gdns. Wig —1C **46**
Thorndale Rd. Thurm —4D **14**
Thorneycroft Clo. B Ast
                —3D **60**
Thornhills. Nar —1C **42**
Thornhills Gro. Nar —1C **42**
Thornholme Clo. Leic —1G **19**
Thornton Clo. B Ast —3C **60**
Thornton Dri. Nar —1F **43**
Thornton La. Mark —6A **8**
Thornton Wlk. Leic —4B **4**
Thornville Clo. Leic —4G **21**
Thorpe Dri. Wig —5F **37**
Thorpe Field Dri. Thurm
                —3D **14**
Thorpe La. Bark —4G **15**

Thorpe St. Leic —2H **27**
Thorpewell. Leic —1H **29**
Threadgold Clo. Leic —5B **12**
Thresher's Wlk. E Gos —2H **7**
Thurcaston Rd. Leic —4D **12**
(in three parts)
Thurcroft Clo. Glen P —6G **35**
Thurlaston La. Cft —4E **41**
Thurlaston La. Earl S & Thurl
—2A **40**
Thurlaston La. End —6D **32**
Thurlby Rd. Leic —6F **21**
Thurlington Rd. Leic —4E **27**
Thurlow Clo. Oad —5D **38**
Thurlow Rd. Leic —6C **28**
Thurmaston Boulevd. Leic
(in three parts) —1H **21**
Thurmaston Footpath. Leic
—1G **21**
Thurmaston La. Leic & Hum
—1H **21**
Thurnby Hill. Leic —2E **31**
Thurnby La. Stoug —6E **31**
Thurn Ct. Leic —6D **22**
Thurncourt Clo. Leic —6C **22**
Thurncourt Gdns. Scrap
—6F **23**
Thurncourt Rd. Leic —6C **22**
Thurnview Rd. Leic —4C **30**
Tichborne St. Leic —3D **28**
Tigers Clo. Wig —1F **45**
Tigers Rd. Wig —1E **45**
Tilford Cres. Leic —1D **44**
Tillett Rd. Braun —5B **26**
Tilley Clo. Leic —6A **26**
Tilling Rd. Leic —2G **19**
Tilling Wlk. Leic —1G **19**
Tilton Dri. Oad —4A **38**
Timber St. Wig —2F **45**
Timberwood Dri. Grob —3E **17**
Tinkers Dell. E Gos —1H **7**
Tiptree Clo. Leic —3H **19**
Tithe St. Leic —6G **21**
Tithings, The. Kib —4A **62**
Tiverton Av. Leic —3E **21**
Tiverton Clo. Nar —3C **42**
Tiverton Clo. Oad —4C **38**
Tiverton M. Leic —3E **21**
Tofts, The. Wig —2B **46**
Tolcarne Rd. Leic —5C **22**
Tolchard Clo. Leic —2A **30**
Tollemache Av. Leic —3A **20**
Toller Rd. Leic —6E **29**
Tollwell Rd. Leic —6C **12**
Tolton Rd. Leic —1H **51**
Tomlin Rd. Leic —4G **21**
Tomlinson Ct. Oad —3A **38**
Tom Paine Clo. Braun —5B **26**
Topcliffe Wlk. Leic —2A **20**
Top Clo. Braun —6B **26**
Tophall Dri. Count —2E **55**
Torcross Clo. Glen —5C **18**
Toronto Clo. Leic —6C **20** (1F **4**)
Torridon Clo. Leic —2H **19**
Torrington Clo. Wig —3B **46**
Torver Ho. Leic —6G **35**
Totland Rd. Leic —5G **19**
Tournament Rd. Glen —6A **18**
Tovey Cres. Leic —5H **35**

Towers Clo. Kir M —3E **25**
Towers Dri. Kir M —3E **25**
Tower St. Leic —3B **28** (7D **5**)
Towle Rd. Leic —5C **18**
(in two parts)
Town End Clo. Leic —1E **37**
Townsend Clo. B Ast —2D **60**
Townsend Clo. Leic —6B **14**
Townsend Ct. Leic —3G **35**
Townsend Rd. End —6H **33**
Townsend Rd. Sto S —4B **50**
Town Sq. Shopping Cen. Sys
—5F **7**
Town St. Bur O —3H **49**
Towpath Link. Wig —3G **45**
Trafalgar Way. Glen P —2D **44**
Trafford Rd. Leic —6H **21**
Tranter Pl. Leic —3F **21**
Treasure Clo. Glen —6A **18**
Treaty Rd. Glen —6B **18**
Tredington Rd. Glen —4B **18**
Treetops Clo. Leic —6A **22**
Trefoil Clo. Leic —3C **22**
Tremaine Dri. Wig —2A **46**
Trenant Rd. Leic —5A **36**
Trent Av. Leic —4C **12**
Trent Clo. B Ast —1C **60**
Trent Clo. Oad —4D **38**
Trescoe Rise. Leic —2C **26**
Tressell Way. Braun —5B **26**
Trevanth Rd. Leic —2H **21**
Trevino Dri. Leic —6C **14**
Trevose Gdns. Leic —6D **22**
Trigo Clo. Leic —1E **19**
Trinity Clo. Sys —6F **7**
Trinity La. Leic —3B **28** (6D **5**)
Trinity Rd. Nar —1G **43**
Trinity Rd. Whet —3H **43**
Triumph Rd. Glen —6A **18**
Trojan Way. Sys —1C **14**
Troon Ind. Est. Leic —1H **21**
(in two parts)
Troon Way. Leic —6B **14**
Troon Way Bus. Cen. Leic
—1H **21**
Trueway Rd. Leic —5G **29**
Truro Dri. Wig —2B **46**
Tuckey Clo. Sap —5C **50**
Tudor Clo. Leic —2H **27**
Tudor Dri. Cosb —3F **53**
Tudor Dri. Oad —3B **38**
Tudor Gro. Grob —4E **17**
Tudor Rd. Leic —6H **19**
Tudor Wlk. Leic —2H **27**
Tunstall Cres. Leic —5G **21**
Turnbull Dri. Leic —1D **34**
Turnbury Way. Leic —5G **29**
Turner Rise. Oad —5B **38**
Turner Rd. Leic —6H **21**
Turner St. Leic —3B **28** (7D **5**)
Turner Wlk. Leic —2A **30**
Turn St. Sys —5E **7**
Turville Clo. Wig —3C **46**
Turville Rd. Leic —4F **27**
Tuskar Rd. Leic —6D **22**
Tuxford Rd. Leic —2A **22**
Twickenham Rd. Leic —1C **44**
Twitten, The. Glen P —2D **44**
Twycross St. Leic —2E **29**

Tyers Clo. Thurl —6A **32**
Tyes End. Leic —2E **19**
Tyler Rd. Rat —5D **16**
Tyndale St. Leic —3H **27**
Tynedale Clo. Oad —4D **38**
Tyringham Rd. Wig —1C **46**
Tyrrell St. Leic —1H **27**
Tysoe Hill. Glen —4B **18**
Tythorn Dri. Wig —5C **36**

Udale Ho. Leic —6G **35**
Ullwater Dri. Oad —4C **38**
Ullswater St. Leic
—3A **28** (7A **5**)
Ullswater Wlk. Oad —4D **38**
Ulvercroft Way. Mark —2C **8**
Ulverscroft Dri. Grob —3F **17**
Ulverscrott La. New L —1G **9**
Ulverscroft Rd. Leic —5D **20**
Una Av. Leic —1E **35**
Underwood Cres. Sap —5C **50**
Underwood Dri. Sto S —4A **50**
Unicorn Mobile Home Pk.
Thurm —3B **14**
Unicorn St. Thurm —3B **14**
Unity Rd. Glen —5A **18**
University Clo. Sys —6F **7**
University Rd. Leic
—5C **28** (8F **5**)
Upland Clo. Mark —2B **8**
Upland Dri. Mark —2B **8**
Uplands Rd. Leic —4B **36**
Uplands Rd. Oad —3R **38**
Up. Brown St. Leic
—2B **28** (5C **5**)
Up. Charnwood St. Leic
—1D **28**
Up. Church St. Sys —5F **7**
Up. George St. Leic
—6C **20** (1E **4**)
Up. Hall Clo. Leic —5C **22**
Up. Hall Grn. Leic —5C **22**
Up. King St. Leic
—3B **28** (7D **5**)
Up. Nelson St. Leic
—3C **28** (6F **5**)
Up. New Wlk. Leic —3D **28**
Up. Temple Wlk. Leic —2E **19**
(in two parts)
Up. Tichborne St. Leic —3D **28**
Upperton Rise. Leic —3G **27**
Upperton Rd. Leic —3G **27**
Uppingham Clo. Leic —2C **30**
Uppingham Dri. B Ast —5H **51**
Uppingham Rd. Leic —6F **21**
Upton Dri. Wig —1D **46**
Utah Clo. Glen —6A **18**
Uttoxeter Clo. Leic —6B **14**
Uxbridge Rd. Leic —1E **21**

Vale Clo. Leic —6C **22**
Vale End. Thurn —2E **31**
Valence Rd. Leic —4F **27**
Valentine Dri. Oad —3H **37**
Valentine Rd. Leic —2D **30**
Valiant Clo. Glen —6B **18**
Valjean Cres. Leic F —4E **25**

Valley Dri. Leic —5A **26**
(in two parts)
Valley Rd. Leic —1B **22**
Valley Rd. Mark —3C **8**
Vancouver Rd. Leic —6C **20**
Vandyke Rd. Oad —5B **38**
Vann Wlk. Leic —3C **20**
Vaughan Rd. Leic —2A **36**
Vaughan St. Leic —1H **27**
Vaughan Way. Leic
—1A **28** (3B **4**)
Ventnor Rd. Leic —2F **37**
Ventnor Rd. S. Leic —3F **37**
Ventnor St. Leic —2F **29**
Verdale Av. Leic —6D **14**
Vernon Rd. Leic —2A **36**
Vernon St. Leic —1H **27**
Vestry Ho. Leic —1C **28** (3E **4**)
Vestry St. Leic —1C **28** (3E **4**)
Vetch Clo. Nar —3B **42**
Vicarage Clo. Kir M —1E **25**
Vicarage Clo. Sys —5F **7**
Vicarage La. Bark —3H **15**
Vicarage La. Belg —2C **20**
Vicarage La. Hum —6B **22**
Vicarage La. Whet —3H **43**
Victoria Av. Leic —3D **28**
Victoria Ct. Oad —2H **37**
Victoria Dri. Grob —3F **17**
Victoria Gdns. Leic —4E **29**
Victoria Pde. Leic —3D **4**
Victoria Pk. Rd. Leic —5C **28**
Victoria Pas. Leic
—3C **28** (6F **5**)
Victoria Rd. Whet —3H **43**
Victoria Rd. E. Leic —5G **21**
Victoria Rd. N. Leic —2C **20**
Victoria St. Flec —6B **58**
Victoria St. Nar —3E **43**
Victoria St. Sys —6F **7**
Victoria St. Thurm —3C **14**
Victoria St. Wig —6F **37**
Victoria Ter. Leic —4D **28**
Victor Rd. Glen —5B **18**
Victors Clo. Leic —5G **35**
Viking Rd. Wig —5C **36**
Villas, The. Kib —4A **62**
Villiers Hall. Oad —1H **37**
Vincent Clo. Leic —1F **27**
Vineries, The. Count —2D **54**
Vine St. Leic —1A **28** (2B **4**)
Vostock Clo. Leic —2D **28**
Vulcan Rd. Leic —1D **28**

Waddesdon Wlk. Leic —5F **21**
Wade St. Leic —2B **20**
Waingrove Wlk. Leic —1B **20**
Wakefield Pl. Leic —3F **21**
Wakeley Clo. Nar —4C **42**
Wakerley Ct. Leic —1F **29**
Wakerley Rd. Leic —4H **29**
Wakes Clo. Dun B —5F **61**
Wakes Rd. Wig —6F **37**
Walcote Rd. Leic —3G **21**
Waldale Dri. Leic —5F **29**
Waldron Dri. Oad —4C **38**
Wale Rd. Whet —4H **43**
Wales Orchard. Leir —6A **60**

Walker Rd. Bir —5F **13**
Walker Rd. Thurm —5D **14**
Walkers Way. Sys —5F **7**
Wallace Ct. Leic —6F **29**
Wallace Dri. Grob —6G **9**
Wallingford Rd. Leic —3B **20**
Wallis Clo. Thurc —1B **12**
Walnut Av. Bir —3F **13**
Walnut Clo. B Ast —1B **60**
Walnut Clo. Mark —3B **8**
Walnut Clo. Oad —4A **38**
Walnut Gro. Glen P —5F **35**
Walnut Leys. Cosb —3F **53**
Walnut St. Leic —4A **28** (8C **5**)
Walnut Way. Blab —5B **44**
Walnut Way. Count —1E **55**
Walpole Ct. Leic —2D **26**
Walsgrave Av. Leic —3D **30**
Walshe Rd. Leic —1B **30**
Walsingham Cres. Leic F
　　　　　　—4H **25**
Waltham Av. Leic —5E **27**
Walton Clo. Kir M —3F **25**
Walton St. Leic —4G **27**
Wand St. Leic —4C **20**
Wanlip Av. Bir —4G **13**
Wanlip La. Bir —4H **13**
Wanlip Rd. Sys —6B **6**
Wanlip St. Leic —6C **20**
Wansbeck Gdns. Leic —5C **22**
Wanstead Rd. Leic —2G **25**
Wanstead Rd. Ind. Pk. Leic F
　　　　　　—2G **25**
Ward Clo. Leic —2G **35**
Wardens Wlk. Leic F —4H **25**
Wards Closes. Wig —3C **46**
Wareham Rd. Blab —5B **44**
Waring Clo. Glen —4C **18**
War Memorial App. Leic
　　　　　　—4C **28** (8F **5**)
Warmsley Av. Wig —5E **37**
Warner Clo. Whet —6A **44**
Warren Av. Leic —6E **15**
Warren Clo. Leic —5A **22**
Warren Clo. Mark —3C **8**
Warren Dri. Leic —6E **15**
Warren La. Leic F —6E **25**
Warren Rd. Nar —2F **43**
Warren St. Leic —1H **27**
Warren, The. E Gos —2H **7**
Warren View. Leic —6E **15**
Warrington Dri. Grob —3E **17**
Warrington St. Leic
　　　　　　—1A **28** (2A **4**)
Warwick Rd. B Ast —5H **51**
Warwick Rd. Kib —5F **59**
Warwick Rd. L'thrpe & Wet
　　　　　　—5E **43**
Warwick Rd. Wig —6D **36**
Warwick St. Leic —1H **27**
Washbrook La. Gt G —2G **49**
Watchcrete Av. Quen —4H **7**
Waterfield Clo. Leic —2B **30**
Waterfield Rd. Crop —1H **11**
Watergate l a. Leic —2B **30**
Waterloo Cres. Count —2D **54**
Waterloo Cres. Wig —6G **37**
Waterloo Way. Leic
　　　　　　—4B **28** (8D **5**)

Watermead Way. Leic —1C **20**
Waterside Rd. Ham —2A **22**
Watery Ga. La. Thurl —3D **40**
　(in two parts)
Watling St. Leic —6B **20** (1C **4**)
Watson Rd. Leic —3E **21**
Watts Clo. Leic —2E **19**
Waudby Clo. L'thrpe —5E **43**
Waveney Rise. Oad —3D **38**
Waverley Rd. Blab —5C **44**
Waverley Rd. Wig —1F **45**
Wavertree. Leic —1E **37**
Wavertree Clo. Cosb —1F **53**
Wayfarer Dri. E Gos —1H **7**
Wayne Way, The. Bir —4G **13**
Wayne Way, The. Leic —1H **29**
　(in three parts)
Wayside Dri. Oad —3C **38**
Wayside Dri. Thurm —5B **14**
Weaver Rd. Leic —6D **22**
Weaver's Wynd. E Gos —2H **7**
Webb Clo. Leic F —5H **25**
Webbs Way. Sto S —3B **50**
Webster Rd. Leic —3C **26**
Weighbridge Ho. Wig —4B **46**
Weir Rd. Kib —5A **62**
Welbeck Av. Leic —3A **20**
Welbeck Clo. Blab —5C **44**
Welcombe Av. Leic —6D **26**
Welcome Stranger Caravan Pk.
　　　　　Sys —5F **7**
Weldon Rd. Wig —5F **37**
Welford Ct. Leic —2D **36**
Welford Pl. Leic —2B **28** (5C **5**)
Welford Rd. Blab —3B **44**
Welford Rd. Leic
　　　　　　—2B **28** (5C **5**)
Welford Rd. Wig & Fos
　　　　　　—1B **46**
Welham Wlk. Leic —1H **21**
Welland St. Leic —3D **28**
Welland Vale Rd. Leic —3C **30**
Wellesbourne Dri. Glen —4B **18**
Welles St. Leic —1A **28** (3A **4**)
Wellgate Av. Bir —3F **13**
Wellhouse Clo. Wig —3A **46**
Wellinger Way. Leic —3C **26**
Wellington St. Leic
　　　　　　—2B **28** (5D **5**)
Wellington St. Sys —6E **7**
Wells Av. Kilb —2D **56**
Well Spring Clo. Wig —3C **46**
Wembley Rd. Leic —2H **25**
Wembury Gdns. Leic —1A **20**
Wendy's Clo. Leic —6D **22**
Wenlock Way. Leic —2A **22**
Wensleydale Rd. Wig —2D **46**
Wensley Rise. Leic —1C **44**
Wentbridge Rd. Leic —2F **21**
Went Rd. Bir —5G **13**
Wentworth Grn. Kir M —3D **24**
Wentworth Rd. Flec —6C **58**
Wentworth Rd. Leic —1G **27**
Wesley Clo. Rat —5C **16**
Wesley Clo. Sap —6C **50**
Wesley St. Leic —2B **20**
Wesley Way. Mark —3C **8**
Wessex Dri. Leic —2C **26**

West Av. Leic —5D **28**
West Av. Wig —5D **36**
Westbourne St. Leic —5C **20**
Westbridge. Leic
　　　　　　—2A **28** (4A **4**)
Westbury Rd. Leic —6C **28**
Westcotes Dri. Leic —3G **27**
West Ct. Leic —3C **28** (7F **5**)
Westdale Av. Glen P —1A **44**
Westdown Dri. Thurm —6C **14**
West Dri. Leic —5A **22**
Westerby Clo. Wig —5F **37**
Westerdale Rd. Wig —1D **46**
Western Av. Flec —6B **58**
Western Boulevd. Leic
　　　　　　—2A **28** (5A **5**)
Western Dri. Blab —4B **44**
Westernhay Rd. Leic —6E **29**
Western Pk. Rd. Leic —2E **27**
Western Rd. Leic —4H **27**
Westfield Av. Count —1D **54**
Westfield Av. Wig —5D **36**
Westfield Rd. Leic —2E **27**
Westgate Av. Bir —3E **13**
Westgate Rd. Leic —3D **36**
Westhill Rd. Leic —2E **27**
W. Holme St. Leic —2H **27**
W. Langton Rd. Kib —6C **62**
Westleigh Av. Leic —4G **27**
Westleigh Bus. Pk. Blab
　　　　　　—2B **44**
Westleigh Rd. Glen P —2E **45**
Westleigh Rd. Leic —4G **27**
Westmeath Av. Leic —1B **30**
Westminster Dri. Glen P
　　　　　　—2D **44**
Westminster Rd. Leic —6G **29**
Westmorland Av. Leic —3E **21**
Westmorland Av. Wig —1F **45**
Weston Clo. Oad —5E **39**
Westover Rd. Leic —5B **26**
　(in two parts)
West St. Blab —3A **44**
West St. Glen —4A **44**
West St. Leic —3B **28** (7D **5**)
West St. Nar —1D **42**
West St. Sys —6E **7**
West St. Open. Leic —3H **27**
Westview Av. Glen P —6F **35**
West Wlk. Leic —3C **28** (7F **5**)
　(in two parts)
Wetherby Clo. Quen —3H **7**
Wetherby Rd. Leic —1F **21**
Wexford Clo. Oad —5D **38**
Weymouth Clo. Wig —3B **46**
Weymouth St. Leic —5D **20**
Wharf St. Thurm —3B **14**
Wharf St. N. Leic
　　　　　　—6C **20** (1E **4**)
Wharf St. S. Leic
　　　　　　—1C **28** (1E **4**)
Wharf Way. Glen P —1B **44**
Wheatfield Clo. Glen —6A **18**
Wheatland Clo. Oad —4D **38**
Wheatland Rd. Leic —6D **12**
Wheatlands Dri. Count —1D **54**
Wheatley Rd. Leic —1H **19**
Wheatleys Rd. Thurm —4B **14**
Wheat St. Leic —1C **28** (2E **4**)

Wheeldale. Wig —1D **46**
Wheeldale Clo. Leic —2H **19**
Whetstone Gorse La. Whet
　　　　　　—3A **54**
Whiles La. Bir —4H **13**
Whinchat Rd. Leic —1E **29**
　(in two parts)
Whinham Av. B Ast —6H **51**
Whistle Way. Nar —3B **42**
Whiston Clo. Leic —6D **22**
Whitby Clo. B Ast —5A **52**
Whiteacres. Whet —6G **43**
White Barn Dri. Cosb —2E **53**
Whitebeam Clo. Nar —3C **42**
White Clo. B Ast —1C **60**
Whitecroft Clo. Mark —3C **8**
Whitefield Rd. Leic —2B **20**
Whitehall Rd. Leic —3B **30**
Whitehead Cres. Wig —6E **37**
White Horse La. Bir —5H **13**
White Ho. Clo. Grob —2E **17**
White Ho. Clo. Leir —6A **60**
Whiteoaks Rd. Oad —6C **38**
Whitesands Clo. Glen —4B **18**
White St. Kib —5H **59**
Whitley Clo. Leic —5F **19**
Whitman Clo. Leic —1B **26**
Whitteney Dri. Leic —5G **35**
Whittier Rd. Leic —2B **36**
Whittington Dri. Rat —4C **16**
Whittle Clo. Whet —5H **43**
Whitwell Row. Leic —4A **36**
Whitwick Rd. Mark —1B **8**
Whitwick Way. Leic —5G **19**
Wicken Rise. Wig —5G **37**
Wickham Rd. Oad —5B **38**
Wicklow Dri. Leic —1A **30**
Wightman Clo. Sto S —2B **50**
Wigley Rd. Leic —5C **22**
Wigston La. Leic —3G **35**
Wigston Rd. Blab —3B **44**
Wigston Rd. Oad —5H **37**
Wigston St. Count —1F **55**
Wigston St. Leic
　　　　　　—2C **28** (4E **4**)
Wilberforce Rd. Leic —4H **27**
William Peardon Ct. Wig
　　　　　　—6E **37**
William Rowlett Hall. Leic
　　　　　　—3A **28** (6A **5**)
William St. Leic —1D **28** (3F **4**)
William St. Nar —4D **42**
Willoughby Gdns. Leic F
　　　　　　—4G **25**
Willoughby Rd. Ash M —5G **61**
Willoughby Rd. Count —2C **54**
Willowbrook Clo. B Ast
　　　　　　—6B **52**
Willow Brook Clo. Glen —3A **18**
Willow Brook Rd. Leic —6E **21**
Willowbrook View. Leic —1E **31**
Willow Clo. Nar —5E **43**
Willow Ct. Leic —2D **28**
Willow Ct. Leic —2D **34**
　(Osiers, The.)
Willow Dri. Count —1E **55**
Willow Dri. Grob —3E **17**
Willow Pk. Dri. Wig —6E **37**

Willow Pl. Wig —1B **46**
Willow Rd. Blab —4B **44**
Willow St. Leic —6C **20**
Willow Tree Clo. Ham —3C **22**
Willow Wlk. Sys —6D **6**
Willsmer Clo. B Ast —2C **60**
Wilmington Ct. Oad —1G **37**
Wilmington Rd. Leic —4G **27**
Wilmore Cres. Leic —4B **26**
Wilne St. Leic —3E **29**
Wilnicott Rd. Leic —6D **26**
Wilsford Clo. Wig —3A **46**
Wilshere Clo. Kir M —2D **24**
Wilson Clo. Braun —5B **26**
Wilson Rd. Wig —2E **45**
Wilson St. Leic —1E **29**
Wilton Clo. Oad —4C **38**
Wilton St. Leic —6B **20** (1D **4**)
Wiltshire Ho. Leic —3H **19**
Wiltshire Rd. Leic —3H **19**
Wiltshire Rd. Wig —5D **36**
Wimbledon St. Leic
—1C **28** (3F **4**)
Wimborne Clo. Wig —2A **46**
Wimbourne Rd. Leic —3F **37**
Winchendon Clo. Leic —6G **21**
Winchester Av. Blab —3A **44**
Winchester Av. Leic —4F **27**
Winchester Rd. Blab —4C **44**
Windermere Dri. Cft —1H **61**
Windermere Rd. Wig —6H **37**
Windermere St. Leic
—4A **28** (7B **5**)
Winders Way. Leic —4H **35**
Windley Rd. Leic —3B **36**
Windmill Av. Bir —3H **13**
Windmill Bank. Wig —2C **46**
Windmill Clo. Rat —6D **16**
Windmill Clo. Thurm —3D **14**
Windmill Gdns. Kib —3A **62**
Windmill Rise. Grob —2E **17**
Windrush Dri. Oad —3D **38**
Windsor Av. Glen P —2E **45**
Windsor Av. Grob —3E **17**
Windsor Av. Leic —3C **20**
Windsor Clo. Oad —6C **38**
Winforde Cres. Leic —3B **26**
Wingfield St. Leic —3D **20**
Winifred St. Leic
—3A **28** (7B **5**)

Winslow Dri. Wig —5G **37**
Winslow Grn. Leic —5C **22**
Winstanley Dri. Leic —3D **26**
Winster Dri. Thurm —3C **14**
Winston Av. Cft —1H **51**
Winterburn Gdns. Whet
—4H **43**
Winterfield Clo. Glen —6H **17**
Wintersdale Rd. Leic —1C **30**
Winterton Clo. Thurm —3D **14**
Winton Av. Leic —5G **27**
Winton Wlk. Leic —5G **27**
Wistow Clo. Kllb —2E **57**
Wistow Rd. Kilb & New H
(in two parts) —2E **57**
Wistow Rd. Wig —2B **46**
Withcote Av. Leic —1B **30**
Withens Clo. Leic —6E **19**
Witherdell. Leic —2E **19**
Withers Way. Leic —5B **26**
Woburn Clo. Leic —5G **35**
Woburn Clo. Wig —1C **46**
Wokingham Av. Leic —1D **44**
Wolds, The. E Gos —1H **7**
Wollaton Clo. Glen —4F **21**
Wolsey Clo. Flec —5B **58**
Wolsey Clo. Grob —3E **17**
Wolsey Clo. Leic F —5F **25**
Wolsey Dri. Rat —4B **16**
Wolsey La. Flec —5B **58**
Wolsey St. Leic —5A **20**
Wolsey Way. Sys —6D **6**
Wolverton Rd. Leic —5G **27**
Woodbank. Glen P —1B **44**
Woodbank Rd. Grob —2D **16**
Woodbank Rd. Leic —3E **37**
Woodbine Av. Leic —3D **28**
Woodborough Rd. Leic —3A **30**
Woodboy St. Leic —6C **20**
Woodbridge Rd. Leic —2D **20**
Woodbury Rise. Gt G —2E **49**
Woodcote Rd. Leic —2C **34**
Woodcroft Av. Leic —3C **36**
Wood End. Leic —6E **19**
Woodfield Clo. Nar —3D **42**
Woodfield Rd. Oad —2B **38**
Woodford Clo. Wig —3A **46**
Woodgate. Leic —6H **19**
Woodgate Dri. Bir —3F **13**
Woodgon Rd. Ans —5F **11**

Woodgreen Rd. Leic —4F **21**
Woodgreen Wlk. Leic —4F **21**
Woodhall Clo. Leic —2B **26**
Wood Hill. Leic —1E **29**
Woodhouse Clo. Mark —3C **8**
Woodhouse Rd. Nar —3C **42**
Woodland Av. Leic —6E **29**
Woodland Av. Nar —2D **42**
Woodland Clo. Mark —3C **8**
Woodland Dri. Leic —5B **26**
Woodland Rd. Leic —6F **21**
Woodlands Dri. Grob —2D **16**
Woodlands La. Kir M —1E **25**
Woodlands, The. Count
—1D **54**
Woodlands, The. Wig —5H **37**
Woodley Rd. Rat —5C **16**
Woodman's Chase. E Gos
—2H **7**
Woodnewton Dri. Leic —3D **30**
Woodpecker Dri. Leic F
—5E **25**
Woods Clo. Oad —3C **38**
Woodshawe Rise. Leic —4C **26**
Woodside Clo. Leic —4F **21**
Woodside Clo. Nar —3B **42**
Woodside Rd. Oad —6D **38**
Woodstock Clo. Leic —1A **20**
Woodstock Rd. Leic —1A **20**
Wood St. Leic —6B **20** (1D **4**)
Woodville Gdns. Wig —4E **37**
Woodville Rd. Leic —2F **27**
Wooldale Clo. Ans —4G **11**
Woolsthorpe Wlk. Leic —5G **21**
Wootton Clo. Whet —5H **43**
Wootton Rise. Leic —4H **35**
Worcester Av. Bir —2H **13**
Worcester Dri. Wig —1F **45**
Worcester Rd. Leic —2H **35**
Wordsworth Cres. Nar —2C **42**
Wordsworth Rd. Leic —1C **36**
Worrall Clo. Leic —3B **26**
Worrall Rd. Leic —3B **26**
Worsley Way. Whet —5A **44**
Worthington St. Leic —2E **29**
Wranglands, The. Flec —6C **58**
Wreake Rd. Thurm —2C **14**
Wreford Cres. Leic —6E **23**
Wren Clo. Leic —2A **36**
Wren Clo. Sys —5C **6**

Wright Clo. Whet —1H **53**
Wright La. Oad —5E **39**
Wroxall Way. Leic —5G **19**
Wyatt Clo. Leic —3A **26**
Wych Elm Clo. Gt G —2D **48**
Wychwood Rd. Whet —6A **44**
Wycliffe St. Leic
—2B **28** (4C **4**)
Wycombe Rd. Leic —5H **21**
Wyedean Dri. Wig —1C **46**
Wykeham Clo. Blab —5B **44**
Wylam Clo. Leic —5F **19**
Wymar Clo. Leic —2G **19**
Wyndale Dri. Sys —4F **7**
Wyndale Rd. Leic —2D **36**
Wyndham Clo. Oad —2C **38**
Wynfield Rd. Leic —2F **27**
Wyngate Dri. Leic —3F **27**
Wynthorpe Rise. Leic —3E **27**
Wynton Clo. Blab —5C **44**
Wyvern Av. Leic —2F **21**
Wyvern Clo. B Ast —2C **60**
Wyville Row. Leic —6E **27**

Yardley Dri. Leic —4D **36**
Yarmouth St. Leic
—6B **20** (1D **4**)
Yarrow Clo. Ham —4C **22**
Yarwell Dri. Wig —1C **46**
Yaxley Clo. Thurn —1F **31**
Yelverton Av. Leic —4C **30**
Yeoman La. Leic
—1C **28** (3E **4**)
Yeoman's Dale. E Gos —1H **7**
Yeoman St. Leic
—1C **28** (3E **4**)
Yew Clo. Leic F —6E **25**
Yews Rd., The. Oad —3B **38**
Yews, The. Oad —3B **38**
Yew Tree Dri. Leic —1A **26**
York Clo. Glen P —2E **45**
York Rd. Leic —2B **28** (5C **5**)
Yorkshire Rd. Leic —4E **21**
York St. Leic —2C **28** (5D **5**)
Yukon Way. Leic
—6C **20** (1F **4**)

Zetland Wlk. Leic —6E **13**